PEGGY PORSCHEN

BOUTIQUE BAKING

delectable cakes, cupcakes and teatime treats

PHOTOGRAPHY BY
GEORGIA GLYNN SMITH

Quadrille
PUBLISHING

For my darling husband Bryn,
for letting me have my 'pink' cake shop
and for giving it your all and more.

Editorial director Jane O'Shea
Creative director Helen Lewis
Project editor Lisa Pendreigh
Assistant Editor Louise McKeever
Designer Helen Bratby
Photographer Georgia Glynn Smith
Stylist Vicky Sullivan
Production director Vincent Smith
Production controller Aysun Hughes

This edition first printed in 2012 by
Alhambra Editions
Alhambra House
27–31 Charing Cross Road
London WC2H 0LS
www.quadrille.co.uk

This edition produced for The Book People, Hall Wood Avenue, Haydock, St Helens, WA11 9UL

Text, recipes and designs
© 2012 Peggy Porschen
Photography
© 2012 Georgia Glynn Smith
(except page 5 top right, page 67 top centre © Adam Ellis)
Artwork, design and layout
© 2012 Quadrille Publishing Ltd

British Library Cataloguing-in-Publication Data
A catalogue record for this book is available from the British Library.

ISBN: 978 184949 236 2
Printed in China

CONTENTS

WELCOME TO BOUTIQUE BAKING

It is a pleasure to introduce my new book, which is based on delicious recipes from my latest venture, the Peggy Porschen Parlour. After seven successful years of running a bespoke cake design company I have finally fulfilled my lifelong dream of opening my first cake boutique, based in London's beautiful Belgravia. Filled with delicious cakes and confections, complementing blends of artisan teas and coffees, the parlour has often been described as 'cake heaven'.

I have always had a passion for baking exquisite cakes. My earliest childhood memories go back to my very first birthday, sitting next to a beautiful marzipan-covered birthday cake with 'Peggy 1' iced on top. Over the following years, eating birthday cake and baking Christmas cookies with my mum and brother were the annual highlights. I started making my own cakes from the age of 14 and soon I knew that there was nothing I would rather do, so I decided to pursue a career in cakes. Coming from a nation famed for its baking and cake culture, the taste has

always been as important to me as the look of a cake so I enrolled at London's school for culinary arts, Le Cordon Bleu, where I completed the Grand Diplôme de Cuisine et Pâtisserie. I later worked for some of the most renowned pastry kitchens in the UK before launching my own business, Peggy Porschen Cakes, in 2003. The business immediately took off and soon I was making cakes for well-known celebrities, quickly establishing myself as one of London's leading names in cake design. In 2005, I published my first book **Pretty Party Cakes** which won the Gourmand World Cook Book Award for 'Best Entertaining Cook Book'. The company has since gone from strength to strength and if you asked me how many cakes I have made since the beginning, I could not possibly tell you.

Opened in October 2010, the Peggy Porschen Parlour has given me the opportunity to create my first 'ready-to-eat' collection of cupcakes, layer cakes and seasonal bakes. Where previously I created exclusive made-to-order cakes for events, my cakes are now accessible to a wider audience. Those of you

who are familiar with my work are aware of just how much I care about making baked goods look perfectly beautiful. When the opportunity of opening the Parlour came along, I was faced with a tough challenge – to create a collection of everyday cakes and bakes that taste utterly delicious and, at the same time, stand proudly next to exquisite celebration cakes. It took months of test baking, tasting, trial and error, but the hard work was worthwhile. In Summer 2011, less than one year after opening, we were awarded five gold stars by the Guild of Fine Foods Great Taste Awards. The menu at the Parlour is a favourite among our local Belgravia customers, and I take great joy and satisfaction in developing seasonal treats and ideas.

I decided to share a selection of my favourites with you in **Boutique Baking**, the first book inspired by my work at the parlour. Filled with a mouth-watering array of cakes, home-bakes and confections, many ideas are inspired by old-time favourites, such as the Chocolate Battenberg and Morello Cherry Bakewell Tarts, seasonal influences for Christmas and Spring, and

recipes inspired by my German roots such as gorgeous Springerle Cookies and sumptuous Black Forest Cupcakes. I have also added a selection of drinks recipes to complement my confections and inspire perfect tea party menus.

I have taken great care to ensure each recipe is suitable for bakers of all experience levels and have set out to demonstrate that, by using simple tools and easy techniques, one can take a plain cake or cookie and without fuss or expertise give it an utterly charming and professional finish. For the more experienced bakers who cherish a decorative challenge, I have slipped in a few slightly more intricate designs, such as my Gingerbread Village, a beautiful Raspberry & Rose Dome Cake as well as a stunning Christmas cake idea.

Writing this book has helped me to rediscover just how much I love to bake. I find it fun and therapeutic and I truly believe that cakes can make people happy. I hope that you will feel enticed and enjoy baking recipes from this book, and that it will become an invaluable source of inspiration for many years to come. Enjoy!

Peggy

SWEET TREATS

MERINGUE KISSES

PRETTY PASTEL-COLOURED MINI MERINGUES ARE SIMPLE AND YET SO ADORABLE;
THEY ADD A LOVELY TOUCH TO A TABLE FOR ANY OCCASION. DISPLAYED
IN CHIC CANDY JARS, THEY LOOK DELICIOUS. WITH A VERY LONG SHELF LIFE,
THEY ARE THE PERFECT GIFT WHEN WRAPPED IN CELLOPHANE BAGS.

Makes approximately 100 meringues

ingredients

100g egg whites (3 large eggs)
Pinch of salt
100g caster sugar
1 tsp vanilla extract
100g icing sugar, sifted
Pink, blue and yellow liquid food colour

equipment

Basic baking kit (see page 172)
3 large plastic piping bags
3 star piping nozzles

Preheat the oven to 80°C/gas mark ¼. Line two baking trays with greaseproof paper.

Place the egg whites and a pinch of salt into the bowl of an electric mixer and start whisking at high speed. Make sure that the bowl is entirely grease-free before you start, otherwise the egg whites will not whip up properly.

As the egg whites are stiffening, slowly sprinkle the caster sugar into the mix. Stop whisking as the meringue becomes stiffer and glossy; be careful not to overwhisk the mixture.

Add the vanilla extract and slowly fold the icing sugar into the meringue mixture using a rubber spatula.

Separate the meringue mix into three equal parts; keep the first white, mix the second with pink liquid food colour to a pastel pink shade and the third with blue and yellow liquid food colour for a pastel aqua shade.

Place a star nozzle in each of the piping bags then fill each one with a different coloured meringue mixture. Pipe little rosettes onto the baking trays lined with greaseproof paper.

Place the meringues in the preheated oven for between 2–3 hours or until they have fully dried out.

Stored in a dry, airtight container, these mini meringue kisses can last for up to 3 months.

CHOCOLATE CRUNCH CAKE WITH MARSHMALLOWS AND PISTACHIOS

THIS RECIPE WAS INTRODUCED TO THE PARLOUR IN CELEBRATION OF THE ROYAL WEDDING OF WILLIAM AND CATHERINE, AFTER I LEARNT THAT CHOCOLATE FRIDGE CAKE IS WILLIAM'S FAVOURITE DESSERT AND WAS TO BE SERVED AT THE WEDDING BREAKFAST. IT HAS BEEN SO POPULAR AMONGST OUR CUSTOMERS THAT THIS CHOCOLATE CAKE HAS EARNT A SPOT IN THIS BOOK.

Makes one 20cm (8in) square cake

ingredients

200g unsalted butter, softened
600g plain chocolate (minimum 53% cocoa solids), chopped or in buttons
6 tbsp golden syrup
290g Rich Tea biscuits, roughly broken
75g peeled pistachio nuts, roughly chopped
150g peeled hazelnuts, roasted and crushed
90g small pink and white marshmallows

equipment

Basic baking kit (see page 172)
20cm (8in) square cake tin or deep baking tray of a similar size

Line the cake tin or baking tray with greaseproof paper.

Place the butter, chocolate and golden syrup in a large plastic bowl and gently melt in the microwave at a medium heat. Alternatively, place the ingredients in a saucepan and gently melt, stirring occasionally, until smooth.

In a separate bowl, mix the broken biscuits with the chopped and crushed nuts and the marshmallows. Add to the chocolate mixture and stir until well combined.

Pour the cake mixture into the prepared tin or tray, then spread it evenly using a rubber spatula. Chill in the fridge until firm and set. Cut into bars of approximately 2.5cm (1in) thick.

Stored in the fridge, the chocolate crunch cake can last for up to 1 week.

MORELLO CHERRY BAKEWELL TARTS

A MODERN TAKE ON A BRITISH TEATIME FAVOURITE: THE CLASSIC BAKEWELL TART.
TO KEEP WITH THE CHERRY THEME, SIMPLY DECORATE THE TARTS
WITH SUGAR CHERRIES AND PINK FONDANT.

Makes approximately 20 tarts

ingredients

For the sweet pastry
150g unsalted butter, softened
90g caster sugar
30g egg (½ large egg), beaten
200g plain flour
50g ground almonds
Pinch of salt

For the frangipan
115g unsalted butter, softened
115g caster sugar
Finely grated zest of 1 lemon
1 tsp almond extract
1 medium egg
110g ground almonds
40g self-raising flour
Pinch of salt

For the filling
150g good-quality Morello cherry jam

For the decoration
2 tbsp apricot jam, sieved
500g liquid fondant
1 tsp glucose
A small amount of simple sugar syrup
(if required, see pages 61–2)
A small amount of sugar paste
A small amount of royal icing
(see pages 182–3)
Pink, red, green and brown
food colour

equipment

Basic baking kit (see page 172)
20 fluted mini tart tins
Spray oil
Plastic piping bag
Small leaf cutter
Paper piping bags (see page 184)
Sugar thermometer

Preheat the oven to 160°C/gas mark 4.

To make the sweet pastry

Place the butter and caster sugar in a mixing bowl and cream together until just combined: do not to make it too fluffy. Gradually add the beaten egg to the mixture.

Sift the flour, almonds and salt into a separate bowl. Add in batches to the butter mixture until just combined. Wrap the dough in cling film and chill for at least 1 hour.

To make the frangipan

Beat the butter, sugar, lemon zest and almond extract until pale and fluffy. Continue whisking and slowly add the egg.

Sift the almonds, flour and salt into a separate bowl. Add in batches to the butter mix until just combined.

To assemble the tarts

Roll out the pastry to a thickness of 2–3mm. Place it into lightly greased tart tins. Fill the bottoms of the cases with 1 teaspoon of cherry jam. Chill for 30 minutes.

Place the frangipan into a piping bag and fill the tart cases to just below the top edge. Make sure you leave a little room at the top as the frangipan will expand during baking.

Bake in a preheated oven for about 15–20 minutes, until the tops are brown and the frangipan is cooked through. Remove the tarts from the tins while still warm and let cool.

To decorate

Once cool, heat the apricot jam until it is smooth and runny. Brush the jam thinly over the tops of the tarts and leave to set.

Heat the fondant in a small saucepan over a medium heat, but be careful not to let it boil. It should have a dipping temperature of approximately 48–52°C and a thick but runny pouring consistency. Should the consistency be too thick at the correct temperature, dilute it with a little bit of sugar syrup.

Add the glucose and the pink food colour to make a soft pink shade. Place the fondant into a deep bowl that will allow for dipping.

Pick one tart up at a time and hold it upside down, dipping it into the hot fondant up to the fluted edge of the tart shell. Lift out and spin it fast to let the excess fondant drip off and leave to set.

If the first dip is not perfect, double dip it once the first layer has set. Make sure that your fondant is always hot and runny when dipping and reheat from time to time as required.

Mix two thirds of the sugar paste with the red food colouring to create a cherry red shade. Shape into small equal-sized balls with your hands, making 2 balls per tart.

Mix the last third of sugar paste with green food colouring and using a small rolling pin, roll the paste out on a surface dusted with icing sugar until 1–2mm thick. Cut out small leaf shapes and score the centre with the back of a small kitchen knife.

Mix a small amount of the royal icing with brown food colour to a soft-peak consistency (see page 183). Fill a paper piping bag with the brown icing. Snip a small tip off the end of the bag and pipe the cherry stems onto the tarts. Stick the cherries and leaves on top using the remaining brown icing.

ICE CREAM CAKE POPS

I SIMPLY COULDN'T IGNORE THE CURRENT CRAZE FOR CAKE POPS
AND HERE I HAVE COME UP WITH MY OWN VERSION USING DIPPING FONDANT
OR FONDANT PATISSIERE. THE TEXTURE IS SMOOTH AND SHINY,
AND INSTANTLY MELTS IN YOUR MOUTH.

Makes approximately 12 cake pops

ingredients

400g vanilla sponge (½ recipe quantity,
see page 116)
600g soft ganache (see page 105)
12 small ice cream wafer cones
Approximately 1 kg caster sugar or enough to
fill a small bowl
600g liquid fondant (also called
fondant patissiere)
1 tsp glucose
A small amount of simple sugar syrup
(if required, see pages 61–2)
A selection of food colours
Sugar sprinkles

equipment

Basic baking kit (see page 172)
Tray
Rubber gloves (optional)
Plastic piping bag
12 plastic drinking cups
Sugar thermometer

Following the recipe on page 116, make a vanilla sponge. Following the recipe on page 105, make a ganache. Leave to cool until it has a soft buttery texture.

Fill a few small plastic bowls with 1kg caster sugar and compress as much as possible. This will provide a stand for the ice cream cones while the fondant icing sets.

Line a tray with greaseproof paper.

To make the cake balls
Break the sponge cake down into crumbs and place in a mixing bowl. Add the ganache a little at a time and combine until all the cake crumbs stick together. Using your hands, shape into 12 equal-sized balls and place them on the prepared tray. You may want to use rubber gloves when doing this as it is a very messy job. Chill in the freezer until firmly set.

To assemble the cake pops
Place the remaining ganache into a plastic piping bag. Cut 2.5cm (1in) from the tip of the bag. Pipe the ganache into a wafer cone until it just reaches the top. Place one chilled cake ball on top and press down to ensure it sticks to the ganache. Stand the cone in a plastic cup and place it back in the freezer to set. Repeat for all the remaining cones and cake balls.

TO ASSEMBLE THE CAKE POPS, FILL THE WAFER CONES WITH GANACHE AND PRESS A CHILLED CAKE BALL ON TOP. ONCE IT HAS SET, DIP THE CAKE BALL INTO LIQUID FONDANT AND TOP WITH MULTI-COLOURED SUGAR SPRINKLES.

To decorate

Melt the fondant in the microwave on a medium heat until runny. Make sure that it does not boil as it will lose its shine. Stir in the glucose and add some sugar syrup to adjust the consistency if required. You want it to be a thick pouring consistency with a dipping temperature of about 48–52°C. This temperature will ensure that the fondant sets immediately after dipping.

Divide the fondant into equal parts and mix with your chosen food colours. Use small bowls with enough depth for dipping the balls.

Take one cake pop at a time and dip it upside down into the fondant right up until it reaches the edge of the wafer cone. Lift out and spin the remaining fondant off. Top with sugar sprinkles while the fondant is still soft.

Push the cone into the bowl filled with caster sugar and leave it to set. You can place a few cones next to each other but make sure they do not touch.

These cake pops will last for up to 5 days when kept at room temperature. Do not refrigerate as the fondant will melt.

PEGGY'S SIGNATURE MACARONS

THIS RECIPE IS FOR THE MORE EXPERIENCED BAKER AS IT REQUIRES
PATIENCE AND PRECISION. BUT DON'T FEEL PUT OFF, ONCE MASTERED IT IS
SO WORTHWHILE. I USE MY OWN PURPLE RASPBERRY AND ROSE JAM
FOR THE FILLING, BUT YOU CAN CREATE YOUR OWN FLAVOUR COMBINATIONS.

Makes approximately 50 macarons or 100 shells

ingredients

200g ground almonds
200g icing sugar
200g egg whites
200g caster sugar
100ml water
Food colour (optional)

equipment

Basic baking kit (see page 172)
Permanent marker pen
Round piping nozzle, 8mm (½in) in diameter
(I use a No. 12 from Wiltons)
Small heart-shape cookie cutter (optional)
Sugar thermometer
Plastic piping bags

Preheat the oven to 150°C/gas mark 2. Prepare the oven trays for the macarons. Cut sheets of baking parchment to fit a couple of oven trays. Using the fat end of a large round piping nozzle and a small heart-shape cookie cutter as templates, draw circles and hearts on the reverse side of the parchment at even intervals.

In a food processor briefly pulse together the ground almonds and icing sugar until mixed well and sift into a large bowl. Set aside (this is known as a 'tant pour tant').

To make an Italian meringue, place the egg white in a clean, dry bowl. Reserve 1 tablespoon of the egg white to mix with the colouring later on.

Place the caster sugar in a small saucepan with the water. Dissolve the sugar over a medium heat, then bring the sugar syrup to the boil. Using a sugar thermometer, measure the temperature of the syrup. When the syrup reaches 115°C, start to slowly whisk the egg whites. Gradually increasing the whisking speed until the eggs are white and frothy. Once the syrup reaches 121°C, slow down the whisking and carefully pour the hot syrup into the egg whites in a thin steady stream – pour down the side of the bowl so that the syrup does not splash onto the whisk.

Once all the syrup has been incorporated, continue whisking quickly until the meringue has cooled to room temperature; this will take about 5–10 minutes.

Once the meringue has cooled, add your preferred colouring to the reserved tablespoon of egg white and then whisk into the meringue.

FOR A CANDY STRIPE SWIRL, PAINT THREE STRIPES OF FOOD COLOUR DOWN THE INSIDE OF THE NOZZLE BEFORE FITTING IT IN THE BAG, FILLING WITH MIXTURE AND PIPING.

Using the rubber spatula, fold the 'tant pour tant' into the meringue in three batches. Fold gently but thoroughly to ensure the mix is loose and smooth when piped. The amount you fold in here and the consistency you achieve is crucial; you want the mix to be even and fall easily off the spatula, but not so liquid that it does not keep a good round shape when piped.

Place the nozzle into the piping bag. Using a rubber spatula, half fill the piping bag with macaron mixture.

Use a little of the macaron mix to secure the sheets of baking parchment in place; smear a small amount of mixture on each corner of the underside of the sheet.

Using the circles you have drawn as a guide, pipe the small rounds. To finish piping the round, stop applying pressure to the bag and flick the nozzle round in a small circular motion as you pull away. This ensures there will be no peak on top of the macaron.

For the hearts, pipe a blob at the top half of the heart and then drag it down to the bottom. Repeat on the other side. If the mixture is the correct consistency, any small trails should sink back to leave a smooth surface.

Once the macarons are all piped, gently tap the tray on the worksurface to bring any large air bubbles to the surface and pop them with a cocktail stick. Leave the macarons to dry out a little on the surface; about 15–30 minutes in dry conditions. You should be able to gently touch the surface of the macaron without your finger sticking.

As soon as the macarons have a dry skin, place them on the lower shelves in the oven and immediately reduce the heat to 135°C/gas mark 1. If your oven bakes from the top, then place a tray on the shelf above the macarons to prevent the tops from browning too much.

Bake for approximately 15 minutes, turning the trays halfway through the cooking time. The macarons are done when the tops are dry. As soon as they are done, remove the tray from the oven and transfer the baking paper, with the macarons still attached, directly onto a wet tea towel. Leave for a few minutes and then remove the macarons.

Store in an airtight container at room temperature for up to two days or in the freezer for longer. Sandwich with your chosen filling on the day of consumption, and once filled refrigerate for one hour before eating – this helps the macarons to soften and the flavours to develop.

TO MAKE A HEART, PIPE A BLOB AT THE TOP AND DRAG IT DOWNWARDS. REPEAT ON THE OTHER SIDE.

flavours

Raspberry and Rose Colour the macaron mixture with pink food colour. When piping, paint the inside of the nozzle with three thick lines of claret paste food colour to achieve the 'candy stripe' look. Sandwich the shells together with raspberry and rose jam – thicken the jam slightly by heating it for 3–4 minutes in a microwave. Leave the jam to cool a little before spreading.

Chocolate Replace 50g of the almonds with 50g cocoa powder, then proceed as normal with the recipe. If desired, add a little brown food colour to the macaron mixture to achieve a darker colour. Sandwich the shells together with dark chocolate ganache (see page 105).

troubleshooting

Egg whites These should be separated a few days in advance and left uncovered in the fridge to allow some of the moisture to evaporate and strengthen the whites. Bring the egg whites to room temperature before using. If in doubt, add a teaspoon of Meri-White to the egg whites to counteract any 'watery-ness'.

Macaronage This is the stage of folding the 'tant pour tant' into the meringue. The consistency achieved is very important – if the mixture is too stiff then the tops will not be smooth after piping; if the mixture is too liquid then it will not keep a good shape and may produce grease spots on the surface of the macaron after baking. If in doubt, test a little of the mix by dropping a teaspoonful onto the baking tray and pulling a little peak up on the surface. If it is ready, the top should sink back into the surface gradually. If the peak stays there, the mix needs to be folded a little longer. Drying It is important to let your macarons dry on the surface before baking. If you do not let them dry, the tops will not be smooth and produce a good 'foot' on the bottom. If you dry them for too long, they will be smooth but not produce a foot at all.

Baking Every oven is different, so it is important to get to know your own oven and what temperature works best. Generally, a low temperature is important to prevent over-browning of the macarons and a low shelf for the same reason. Some chefs find the macarons can bake too quickly on the bottom and therefore recommend using two trays, one on top of the other, to bake your macarons – I find they can brown on top more easily so tend to place a tray on the rack above instead. If you bake the macarons for too long, they will lift easily off the paper but be a bit dry and possibly over-brown; to counteract the dryness you can place them in an airtight container in the fridge for a day to soften. If they are not baked enough, they will be too soft and not lift off the paper properly; they will also sink back down and develop what look like grease spots on the top.

MINI CINNAMON DOUGHNUTS

THESE ARE LOVELY LITTLE TREATS THAT NOT ONLY LOOK PRETTY AND TASTE YUMMY BUT THEY ARE ALSO LOW IN FAT AS THEY ARE BAKED RATHER THAN FRIED. WHEN PACKAGED IN NICE PRESENTATION BOXES THEY MAKE CUTE GIFTS.

Makes approximately 36 doughnuts

ingredients

110g plain flour
½ tsp baking powder
¼ tsp ground cinnamon
Pinch of salt
65g caster sugar
25g light brown sugar
1 medium egg
45g whole milk
40g buttermilk
½ tsp vanilla extract
15g unsalted butter, melted
600g liquid fondant (also called
fondant patissiere)
1 tsp glucose
A small amount of simple sugar syrup
(if required, see pages 61–2)
A selection of liquid food colours
50g plain chocolate, melted

equipment

Basic baking kit (see page 172)
3 mini doughnut oven trays
Spray oil
Plastic piping bag (optional)
Sugar thermometer

Preheat the oven to 160°C/gas mark 3. Prepare the mini doughnut oven trays by greasing each mould with spray oil.

Sift together the flour, baking powder, ground cinnamon, salt and sugars into a mixing bowl. In a separate bowl whisk together the egg, milk, buttermilk, vanilla extract and melted butter.

Pour the liquid ingredients onto the dry ingredients, mixing briefly until just combined.

Pipe or pour the mix into the prepared trays, filling only just halfway.

Bake for 10–12 minutes or until the tops spring back to the touch and have lightly browned.

Melt the fondant in the microwave on a medium heat until runny. Make sure that it does not boil as the fondant will lose its shine. Stir in the glucose and add some sugar syrup to adjust the consistency, if required. You want it to be a thick pouring consistency. The temperature of the fondant must be about 48–52°C: this ensures that the fondant sets immediately after dipping.

Divide the fondant equally between small, deep bowls and mix with your chosen food colours.

Dip each doughnut upside down into the fondant until half coated. Leave to set slightly then drizzle with the melted chocolate using a teaspoon or fork. Leave to set.

MARSHMALLOW PUFFS

SERVE THESE CHEERING MARSHMALLOW PUFFS WITH A CUP OF HOME-MADE HOT CHOCOLATE (SEE PAGES 164–5). I MADE MINE INTO DOME SHAPES BUT YOU CAN ALSO SPREAD THE MARSHMALLOW ON A TRAY THEN USE COOKIE CUTTERS TO MAKE FUN SHAPES.

Makes approximately 60–70 small puffs

ingredients

280ml water
6 sheets gelatine
620g caster sugar
130g glucose
70g egg whites (approximately 2 large eggs),
at room temperature
Pinch of salt
Seeds of 1 vanilla pod
Pink, purple and green liquid food colour

equipment

Basic baking kit (see page 172)
Sugar thermometer
Plastic piping bags
Silicon trays with dome shape wells of
approximately 4.5cm (1¾in) diameter
Spray oil

Place the gelatine in a saucepan with 130ml of the water. Leave to soak for 10–15 minutes. Gently warm the gelatine until the leaves have dissolved. Alternatively, dissolve the gelatine by microwaving it in short bursts on a low–medium heat.

Place 320g of the caster sugar and the glucose in a small saucepan with the remaining water. Gently warm over a low heat until the sugar has dissolved, then turn up the heat and bring the syrup to the boil.

Using a sugar thermometer, measure the temperature of the syrup. When the syrup reaches 115°C, place the egg whites in a mixing bowl with the dissolved gelatine and salt and start whisking. Once the syrup reaches 121°C, slow down the whisking and carefully pour the syrup into the egg whites in a thin steady stream – pour down the side of the bowl so that the syrup does not splash onto the whisk.

Once all the syrup has been incorporated into the egg whites, continue whisking quickly until the marshmallow has cooled to room temperature. Once the marshmallow has cooled, add the vanilla seeds.

For a combination of colours, divide the mix into equal parts and fold the liquid food colour through with a spatula. Place each coloured mixture into a separate piping bag using a rubber spatula. Cut approximately 2.5cm (1in) from the tip of the bag and pipe the marshmallow into the greased moulds. Leave to dry for several hours.

In the meantime, make the coloured sprinkling sugars. Divide the remaining caster sugar evenly between 3 bowls and mix each with a few drops of liquid food colour, matching the colours of the marshmallows. Sift out any lumps before use.

Once the marshmallows are fully set, remove them from the moulds and roll in their coordinating sprinkling sugars. Leave the marshmallows to dry uncovered overnight before packing into airtight containers. The marshmallows can be stored like this for up to 5 days.

BEAUTIFUL
BISCUITS

CITRUS BUTTERFLY BISCUITS

BEAUTIFUL BUTTERFLIES WITH A FRESH AND ZESTY ZING MAKE THE PERFECT
ACCOMPANIMENT FOR AN AROMATIC CUP OF TEA. THE CLEVER YET
MINIMAL DECORATION LENDS AN INTRICATE HAND-MADE FEEL ADDING
A TOUCH OF FINESSE WITHOUT COMPROMISING TASTE.

Makes approximately 25 biscuits

ingredients

250g unsalted butter, softened
250g caster sugar
Pinch of salt
For orange biscuits
Finely grated zest of 2 oranges
For lemon biscuits
Finely grated zest of 3 lemons
For lime biscuits
Finely grated zest of 3 limes
1 large egg
500g plain flour, plus extra for dusting
Icing sugar, for dusting

equipment

Basic baking kit (see page 172)
Selection of butterfly cookie cutters
Selection of laser-cut cake or cookie stencils,
or alternatively use doilies

Preheat the oven to 175°C/gas mark 3. Line a baking tray with greaseproof paper.

To make the biscuits
Place the butter, sugar, salt and preferred zest in a mixing bowl and cream together until smooth and creamy in texture.

Beat the egg lightly in another bowl and slowly add to the butter mixture while whisking until well incorporated.

Sift in the flour and mix until the dough just comes together. Gather the dough into a ball, wrap in cling film and chill for at least 30 minutes or until the dough feels firm and cool.

Place the dough on a floured surface and knead briefly.

Roll out the dough to a thickness of approximately 3–4mm. Using a selection of butterfly cookie cutters, cut out the butterfly shapes and place them onto the prepared baking tray. Chill again for 30 minutes or until cool and firm.

Bake for 6 minutes or until the biscuits are golden brown around the edges.

Once the biscuits are baked, let them rest for about 30 minutes outside of the oven.

To decorate
Once cool, place either the stencils or the doilies on top of the biscuits. Using a fine sieve, lightly dust the biscuits with icing sugar. Carefully lift the stencils off to reveal the pretty icing sugar patterns.

tip

Always bake biscuits of the same size together on a tray,
otherwise the smaller ones will burn while the larger ones are baking.

SPRINGERLE COOKIES

SPRINGERLE ORIGINATE FROM GERMANY AND ARE TRADITIONALLY MADE USING
HAND-CARVED WOODEN MOULDS. THE RECIPE CONTAINS HARTSHORN SALT
AS A RAISING AGENT, WHICH ALLOWS THEM TO KEEP THEIR SHAPE.
MADE AROUND CHRISTMAS TIME, THEY ARE PERFECT AS TREE DECORATIONS AND GIFTS.
Makes approximately 20 cookies

ingredients

¼ tsp Hartshorn salt (baker's ammonia),
alternatively use baking powder
1 tbsp milk
3 medium eggs
380g icing sugar
Finely grated zest of 1 lemon
50g salted butter, softened
500g plain flour, plus extra for dusting

equipment

Basic baking kit (see page 172)
Selection of wooden Springerle moulds

Make the dough one or two days before baking.

To make the cookies
Place the Hartshorn salt and milk together in a small bowl. Mix and set aside. Please note that the Hartshorn salt will give off a strong smell.

In a separate bowl whisk the eggs until they are thick and frothy and have a slight yellow colour. Gradually add the icing sugar, lemon zest and butter in small chunks, then add the Hartshorn mixture. Continue to mix for a further 30 minutes.

Gradually add the flour. Once the dough becomes too difficult to mix, knead in any remaining flour, a little at a time. The texture should be light and not too sticky. Once the dough reaches the required consistency, don't add any more flour as the dough will harden too fast.

On a floured surface roll out the dough to a thickness of 10–15mm. Press the mould firmly into the dough and lift off. Using a knife, trim any excess dough from the edges of the embossed design. Alternatively, use a cookie cutter if you have one the correct size. For rounds or ovals, trim around the mould on the dough before lifting off to ensure the shape does not tear.

Transfer the cookies onto a baking tray lined with greaseproof paper. Leave them to air dry for 24–48 hours, depending on size.

Preheat the oven to 225°C/gas mark 7 and bake for 15–20 minutes, depending on size, or until the cookies are light golden brown on the bottom but remain white on top. During baking the bases puff up leaving the tops in perfect shape.

These cookies are soft and chewy in texture, however they harden quite quickly. Stored in an airtight container they keep for up to one month or, if for decorative purposes only, they last for several months.

BLOSSOM BISCUITS

THIS IS A VERY QUICK AND EASY WAY TO DECORATE AN OTHERWISE PLAIN BISCUIT, USING A SIMPLE SILICON MOULD TO MAKE SUGAR PASTE BLOSSOMS. MADE IN A SELECTION OF PRETTY COLOURS, THESE COOKIES MAKE FABULOUS PRESENTS OR PARTY FAVOURS.

Makes approximately 30–40 biscuits

ingredients

200g unsalted butter, softened
200g caster sugar
Seeds of 1 vanilla pod
Pinch of salt
1 medium egg
400g plain flour, plus extra
for dusting
600g sugar paste
2 tsp gum tragacanth
Yellow, orange, pink and red paste
food colour
A small amount of white vegetable
fat (optional)
A small amount of apricot jam, sieved

equipment

Basic baking kit (see page 172)
4–5cm (1½–2in) round pastry cutter
Chrysanthemum silicon mould
(I use a mould from
First Impressions)

Preheat the oven to 175°C/gas mark 3. Line two baking trays with greaseproof paper.

To make the biscuits
Place the butter, sugar, vanilla seeds and salt in a mixing bowl and cream together until smooth and creamy in texture.

Beat the egg lightly in another bowl and slowly add to the butter mixture while whisking until well incorporated.

Sift in the flour and mix until the dough just comes together. Gather the dough into a ball, wrap in cling film and chill for at least 30 minutes or until the dough feels firm and cool.

Place the dough on a floured surface and knead briefly. Roll out the dough to a thickness of 4–5mm. Using a round cookie cutter, cut out 30 rounds and place them onto the prepared baking trays. Chill again for 30 minutes or until cool and firm.

Bake for 6 minutes or until the biscuits are golden brown around the edges. Once the biscuits are baked, let them rest for about 30 minutes outside of the oven.

To decorate
Knead the sugar paste with the gum tragacanth until it starts feeling firm and stretchy.

Divide the sugar paste into four equal parts. Mix the first with a small amount of yellow paste food colour to a pale lemon shade, the second with orange to a pale peach shade and the third with pink to a pale pink shade. To create a coral shade, combine a little of the red and orange paste food colours and use to colour the fourth part. If the sugar paste sticks to your fingers while colouring, add a small amout of vegetable fat.

Once the sugar paste is coloured, cover with cling film to prevent it from drying out. Leave to rest for 30 minutes to firm up a little.

Following the instructions on page 175, make a chrysanthemum blossom for each cookie using the different colour sugar pastes.

To stick the blossoms to the tops of the cookies, gently heat the apricot jam in a saucepan. Brush a thin layer of the jam over each cookie then place the blossoms on top. Leave to set.

TEASPOON CHOCOLATE BISCUITS

IT'S ALL IN THE LITTLE DETAILS... A DAINTY CHOCOLATE BISCUIT SPOON CAN ADD THAT SPECIAL TOUCH TO A SIMPLE CUP OF TEA.

Makes approximately 30 biscuits

ingredients

200g unsalted butter, softened
200g caster sugar
Pinch of salt
1 medium egg
350g plain flour, sifted, plus extra for dusting
50g cocoa powder, sifted

equipment

Basic baking kit (see page 172)
Teaspoon cookie cutter (I use one from a
teatime cookie cutter set)

Preheat the oven to 175°C/gas mark 3. Line a baking tray with greaseproof paper.

To make the biscuits
Place the butter, sugar and salt in a mixing bowl and cream together until smooth and creamy in texture.

Beat the egg lightly in another bowl and slowly add to the butter mixture while whisking until well incorporated.

Sift in the flour and cocoa powder and mix until the dough just comes together. Gather the dough into a ball, wrap in cling film and chill for at least 30 minutes or until the dough feels firm and cool.

Place the dough on a floured surface and knead briefly. Roll out the dough to a thickness of approximately 3–4mm. Using a teaspoon cookie cutter, cut out the spoon shapes and place them onto the prepared baking tray. Chill again for 30 minutes or until cool and firm.

Bake for 6 minutes or until the biscuits spring back to the touch. Once the biscuits are baked, let them rest for about 30 minutes outside of the oven.

COOKIE ADVENT CALENDAR

THIS IS A LOVELY IDEA FOR A HOME-MADE ADVENT CALENDAR.
TO HANG ON A WALL, STICK THE COOKIES TO A CAKE BOARD
THAT HAS BEEN COVERED WITH SUGAR PASTE.
ALTERNATIVELY, HANG THE COOKIES WITH RIBBON
ON A CHRISTMAS TREE OR WREATH.

Makes approximately 24 cookies

ingredients

1 recipe quantity of gingerbread dough
(see page 48)
Plain flour, for dusting
600g royal icing
(see pages 182–3)
Red, green, pink, ivory, black and orange
paste food colour
Edible gold lustre
Small amount of clear alcohol, such as vodka
Small amount of piping gel

equipment

Basic baking kit (see page 172)
Selection of Christmas-themed cookie
cutters (such as Santa Claus, snowman,
snowflake, Christmas tree, sleigh,
bauble, star, candy cane, holly leaf,
stocking) and one square cookie cutter
Paper piping bags (see page 184)
Re-sealable plastic bags
Flat, wide paintbrush

WHEN USING EDIBLE LUSTRE, FIRST ICE THE COOKIE WITH IVORY-COLOURED ICING AS THIS PROVIDES A GOOD BASE FOR THE GOLD POWDER.

Preheat the oven to 180°C/gas mark 4. Line two baking trays with greaseproof paper.

To make the cookies
On a floured surface roll out the gingerbread dough to a thickness of approximately 4–5mm. Using your selection of Christmas-themed cookie cutters, cut out the various shapes and place them onto the prepared baking trays. Chill for at least 30 minutes.

Bake for 6–8 minutes, depending on size, or until the cookies spring back to the touch and are slightly darker around the edges.

Once the cookies are baked, let them rest for about 30 minutes outside of the oven.

To ice the cookies
Following the instructions on page 184, prepare the paper piping bags. You need two piping bags for each colour of icing: one filled with soft-peak icing to pipe the outlines and one filled with runny icing to flood the outlined shapes. Once prepared, keep each piping bag in a re-sealable plastic bag to prevent the icing from drying out between use.

When icing cookies, always outline and flood one colour at a time, allowing the icing to dry completely before adding the next colour to the cookie. This helps to prevent the different colours from bleeding into each other.

For each colour, take the piping bag filled with soft-peak icing and cut a small section from the tip of the piping bag. Trace the outline of the coloured area onto the cookie. Then take the piping bag filled with runny icing in the corresponding colour and use this to flood the centre of the outlined area.

Once all the cookies have been flooded and allowed to dry completely, use the soft-peak icing in various colours to pipe on any additional detail required.

The snowflake cookies are not flooded with icing, instead the detail is piped directly onto the cookies using white soft-peak icing.

To decorate with gold lustre
Ice the cookies with ivory coloured icing and leave to dry. This provides a good base for gold lustre. Mix small amounts of lustre powder, clear alcohol and piping gel to create a thick paste. Using a flat, wide paintbrush, brush the paste all over the ivory icing and leave to dry.

GINGERBREAD VILLAGE

CREATE A CHARMING COLLECTION OF GINGERBREAD HOUSES,
PEOPLE AND SNOWFLAKES TO HANG ON THE CHRISTMAS TREE:
A BEAUTIFUL WINTER-WONDERLAND DISPLAY.

Makes approximately 25–30 cookies, depending on size

ingredients

5 tbsp water
210g light brown sugar
3 tbsp treacle
3 tbsp golden syrup
3 tbsp ground ginger
3 tbsp ground cinnamon
1 tsp ground cloves
250g salted butter, cold and diced
1 tsp bicarbonate of soda
560g plain flour, plus extra for dusting
½ quantity royal icing (see pages 182–3)

equipment

Basic baking kit (see page 172)
Selection of townhouse, snowflake and
gingerbread man and woman cookie cutters
Small electric drill with drill bit for food use
only, approximately 4mm (¼in) diameter
Laser-cut townhouse stencils
Paper piping bag (see page 184)
Mini candy canes (optional)
Red gingham ribbon, for hanging

Preheat the oven to 200°C/gas mark 6. Line two baking trays with greaseproof paper.

To make the gingerbread
Place the water, brown sugar, treacle, golden syrup, ground ginger, cinnamon and cloves into a deep saucepan. Over a medium heat, bring the mixture to the boil while stirring continuously. Remove from the heat, gradually add the diced butter and stir until combined. Add the bicarbonate of soda: take care as the mixture will swell up at this point. Leave the mixture to cool to room temperature.

Once cool, transfer the mixture to a large bowl. Sift in the flour and slowly mix together to form a slightly wet and sticky dough. Wrap in cling film and chill for 2 hours or until cool and firm.

On a floured surface roll out the gingerbread dough to a thickness of approximately 5–6mm. Using your selection of cookie cutters, cut out

the various house, snowflake, man and woman shapes and place them onto the prepared baking trays. Chill for at least 30 minutes.

Bake for 8–10 minutes, depending on size, or until the cookies spring back to the touch and are slightly darker around the edges.

To make the ribbon holes
Once the cookies are baked, remove from the oven and leave to cool completely. To make the ribbon holes, I use a small electric drill with a clean, sterilised drill bit. Place the cookie on a wire cooling rack, then holding the electric drill vertically, make a small hole in the top of the cookie. This method prevents the cookie from breaking.

Alternatively, while the cookies are still hot, use a tiny round cookie cutter or the tip of a long thin piping nozzle to make the ribbon holes. As the cookies are hot, take care not to burn your fingers when using this method.

To ice the cookies

Following the instructions on page 182, prepare the royal icing, mixing it to a soft-peak consistency. Keep the icing covered with a damp cloth to prevent it from drying out.

To decorate the townhouse cookies, place a stencil on the surface of a cookie, holding it down at one end to prevent it from moving. Using a palette knife, scoop up a small amount of icing and spread it thinly over the stencil, ensuring that all gaps are covered. This appears trickier than it really is, as once the icing touches the stencil it helps to hold it in position. Carefully lift off the stencil and leave the iced cookie to dry. Clean the stencil before using it again.

To decorate the snowflake and gingerbread man and woman cookies, following the instructions on page 184, prepare a paper piping bag. Fill the piping bag with soft-peak consistency royal icing and cut a small section from the tip of the bag. Pipe the outlines and details onto each cookie as preferred. Use the same piping bag to pipe an outline onto the townhouse cookies. While the icing is still wet, stick candy canes to the gingerbread man cookies.

Once all the cookies are decorated and dry, thread pieces of gingham ribbon through the holes. Hang the cookies on a tree to create a pretty winter village display.

tip

Humid or damp conditions can make gingerbread go soft. If the air is too dry, the icing can fall off.

MULLED WINE STARS

THIS SIMPLE YET DELICIOUS BISCUIT RECIPE IS THE PERFECT CHRISTMAS COMFORT FOOD.
ENJOY THEM WITH A GLASS OF MULLED WINE (SEE PAGE 168).
ALTERNATIVELY, THESE TREATS CAN BE FLAVOURED WITH SPICED ORANGE MARMALADE.
Makes approximately 20 biscuits

ingredients

250g unsalted butter, softened
250g caster sugar
1 tsp ground cinnamon
Pinch of salt
1 large egg
500g plain flour,
plus extra for dusting
Icing sugar, for dusting
350g Peggy's Mulled Wine Jam
or any other good-quality spiced
berry jam

equipment

Basic baking kit (see page 172)
One large and one small star
cookie cutter

Preheat the oven to 175°C/gas mark 3. Line a baking tray with greaseproof paper.

To make the biscuits
Place the butter, sugar, cinnamon and salt in a mixing bowl and cream together until smooth and creamy in texture.

Beat the egg lightly in another bowl and slowly add to the butter mixture while whisking until well incorporated.

Sift in the flour and mix until the dough just comes together. Gather the dough into a ball, wrap in cling film and chill for at least 30 minutes or until the dough feels firm and cool.

Place the dough on a floured surface and knead briefly.

Roll out the dough to a thickness of approximately 3–4mm. Using a large star cookie cutter, cut out 30 star shapes and place them onto the prepared baking tray.

Using a small star cookie cutter, cut the centres from 15 of the star shapes. You can re-use the cut-out dough to make a few more stars. Chill again for 30 minutes or until cool and firm.

Bake for 6 minutes or until golden brown around the edges.

Once the biscuits are baked, let them rest for about 30 minutes outside of the oven.

To assemble the biscuits
Gently heat the jam in a saucepan until smooth. Spread one teaspoonful of jam evenly over the whole stars.

Lightly dust the hollow stars with icing sugar and place one on top of each of the whole stars spread with jam.

CUPCAKE HEAVEN

BANOFFEE CUPCAKES

A FAVOURITE AT THE PARLOUR, THIS RECIPE IS A FUSION OF BANANA SPLIT
AND BANOFFEE PIE. A DELICIOUS COMBO OF VANILLA SPONGE
WITH CHUNKY CHOCOLATE CHIPS AND FLUFFY FROSTING, THE SECRET LIES IN THE
SURPRISE FILLING OF CREAMY TOFFEE AND CHOPPED BANANAS.

Makes approximately 24 cupcakes

ingredients

For the decoration
50g white sugar florist paste
Small amount of white vegetable fat
Brown and yellow paste food colour
Small amount of royal icing (see pages 182–3)

For the frosting
200g full-fat cream cheese
200g unsalted butter, softened
500g icing sugar, sifted
50g frozen banana purée (or make your own
by mashing a fresh banana)

For the sponge
200g unsalted butter, softened
200g caster sugar
Pinch of salt
Seeds of 1 vanilla pod
4 medium eggs
200g self-raising flour
70g plain chocolate (minimum 53%
cocoa solids), chopped into small pieces

For the sugar syrup
150ml water
150g caster sugar
Scraped vanilla pod

For the filling
200g dulce de leche or soft caramel
(or make your own by boiling
a can of sweetened condensed milk
submerged in water for 3 hours)
1 large ripe banana

equipment

Basic baking kit (see page 172)
Small non-stick plastic board
Five-petal blossom cutter and veiner
Paper piping bag (see page 184)
Paint palette or perforated foam pad,
to dry blossoms
Two 12-hole muffin trays
24 large brown cupcake cases
Melon baller
Plastic piping bags
Large plain round piping nozzle

To make the decoration

Following the instructions on page 174, make the sugar blossom decorations one day ahead of assembling and serving. Make one blossom per cupcake.

Mix the sugar florist paste with a small amount of vegetable fat and the brown paste food colour to a chocolate brown shade. Mix the royal icing with the yellow paste food colour following the instructions on pages 182–3. Using a blossom cutter and veiner, make 24 sugar blossoms then pipe a yellow centre into each flower. Leave to dry.

Preheat the oven to 175°C/gas mark 4. Prepare the muffin trays by placing the cupcake cases inside the holes.

To make the frosting

Place the cream cheese in a mixing bowl and beat until smooth and creamy.

Place the butter and icing sugar in a separate mixing bowl. Reserve the vanilla pod for the sugar syrup. Cream together until very pale and fluffy.

Add the cream cheese, a little at a time, to the butter mixture and mix at medium–high speed until the frosting is combined. Add the banana purée. Chill until set.

To make the cupcakes

Place the butter, sugar, salt and vanilla seeds in a mixing bowl and cream together until pale and fluffy.

Beat the eggs lightly in another bowl and slowly add to the butter mixture while whisking quickly. If the mixture starts to separate or curdle, stop adding the egg and beat in 2–3 tablespoons of flour. This will rebind the batter.

Once all the egg has been incorporated into the butter mixture, sift in the remaining flour and stir until the batter is just combined. This will ensure the sponges stay light and fluffy. Fold the chopped chocolate through the batter using a rubber spatula.

Using a plastic piping bag or a tablespoon, carefully place the batter into the cupcake cases until two-thirds full only.

Bake for 12–15 minutes, depending on your oven. The cupcakes are cooked when the tops are golden brown and spring back to the touch. If in doubt, insert a clean knife or wooden skewer into the centre of each sponge; it should come out clean.

To make the sugar syrup

While the cupcakes are baking, prepare the sugar syrup for soaking. Place the water, sugar and vanilla pod into a saucepan and bring to the boil. Simmer until all the sugar crystals have dissolved. Set aside to cool down slightly. Discard the vanilla pod.

Once the cupcakes are baked, let them rest for about 10 minutes outside of the oven. Using a pastry brush, soak the tops of the cupcakes with sugar syrup while they are still warm; this allows the syrup to be absorbed faster.

Once just warm, remove the cupcakes from the trays and leave to cool completely on a wire cooling rack.

Once cool, wrap the cupcakes in cling film and then chill for 1 hour or until the sponge feels firm to the touch. Using a melon baller, scoop out the tops of each cupcake.

To add the filling

Using a fork, crush the ripe banana and then mix it together with the dulce de leche. Place the banoffee mixture into a plastic piping bag and use to fill the scooped-out holes of the cupcakes.

To decorate

Following the instructions on page 178, prepare a plastic piping bag fitted with a large plain round nozzle. Fill with the chilled frosting. Pipe a swirl of frosting on top of each cupcake.

To finish, place a sugar blossom on the top of the frosting for each cupcake.

STICKY TOFFEE CUPCAKES

THIS IS THE PARLOUR'S MOST POPULAR CUPCAKE. DUE TO THE GOOEY CARAMEL CENTRE, THIS CAKE IS VERY MOIST. ITS PUDDING-LIKE TEXTURE MAKES IT THE PERFECT COMFORT FOOD FOR COLD AND RAINY AUTUMN DAYS.

Makes approximately 24 cupcakes

ingredients

For the decoration
About 250g marzipan
Small amount of white vegetable fat
Small amount of edible copper
and gold lustre powder

For the frosting
200g full-fat cream cheese
200g unsalted butter, softened
500g icing sugar, sifted
120g dulce de leche or soft caramel
(or make your own by boiling
a can of sweetened condensed milk
submerged in water for 3 hours)

For the cake mix
70ml water
290g dates, pitted and roughly chopped
1½ tsp vanilla extract
130g unsalted butter, softened
240g Muscovado sugar
290g self-raising flour
1½ tsp bicarbonate of soda
3 large eggs
145g walnuts, chopped and toasted

For the sugar syrup
150ml water
150g caster sugar

For the filling
Approximately 250g dulce de leche
or soft caramel (see above)

equipment

Basic baking kit (see page 172)
Autumn leaf silicon mould
(I use a mould from First Impressions)
Large soft brush
Paint palette or perforated foam pad,
to dry leaves
Two 12-hole muffin trays
24 large brown cupcake cases
Plastic piping bags
Large plain round piping nozzle

To make the decoration
Following the instructions on page 177, make the autumn leaf decorations at least one day ahead of assembling and serving. Make one leaf per cupcake.

Preheat the oven to 175°C/gas mark 4. Prepare the muffin trays by placing the cupcake cases inside the holes.

To make the frosting
Place the cream cheese in a mixing bowl and beat until smooth and creamy.

Place the butter and icing sugar in a separate mixing bowl and cream together until very pale and fluffy.

Add the cream cheese, a little at a time, to the butter mixture and mix at medium-high speed until the frosting is combined. Add the dulce de leche. Chill until set.

To make the cupcakes
Place the chopped dates into a mixing bowl and pour over the boiling water. Leave to soak for 20 minutes.

USING A PLAIN ROUND NOZZLE, PIPE A PERFECT SWIRL OF FROSTING ON TO THE TOP OF EACH CUPCAKE BEFORE ADDING THE FINISHING DECORATIONS.

Once soaked, drain the dates and then gently break them up into smaller pieces. Add the vanilla extract to the dates.

Place the butter and sugar in a mixing bowl and cream together until pale and fluffy.

Sift the flour and bicarbonate of soda into a separate bowl and set aside.

Whisk the eggs lightly in another bowl and slowly stir into the butter mixture. If the mixture starts to separate or curdle, stop adding the egg and beat in 2–3 tablespoons of the flour. This will rebind the batter.

Once all the egg has been incorporated into the butter mixture, fold in the remaining flour using a rubber spatula, followed by the soaked dates and chopped walnuts. Stir until the batter is just combined. This will ensure the sponges stay light and fluffy.

Using a plastic piping bag or a tablespoon, carefully place the batter into the cupcake cases until two-thirds full only.

Bake for 15–20 minutes, depending on your oven. The cupcakes are cooked when the tops are golden brown and spring back to the touch. If in doubt, insert a clean knife or wooden skewer into the centre of each sponge; it should come out clean.

To make the sugar syrup
While the cupcakes are baking, prepare the sugar syrup for soaking. Place the water and caster sugar into a saucepan and bring to the boil. Simmer until all the sugar crystals have dissolved. Set aside to cool down slightly.

Once the cupcakes are baked, let them rest for about 10 minutes outside of the oven. Using a pastry brush, soak the tops of the cupcakes with sugar syrup while they are still warm; this allows the the syrup to be absorbed faster.

Once just warm, remove the cupcakes from the trays and leave to cool completely on a wire cooling rack.

Once cool, wrap the cupcakes in cling film and then chill for 1 hour or until the sponge feels firm to the touch. Using a melon baller, scoop out the tops of each cupcake.

To add the filling
Place the dulce de leche into a plastic piping bag and use to fill the scooped-out holes of the cupcakes.

To decorate
Following the instructions on page 178, prepare a plastic piping bag fitted with a large plain round nozzle. Fill with the chilled frosting. Pipe a swirl of frosting on top of each cupcake.

To finish, place a marzipan leaf on the top of the frosting for each cupcake.

BLACK FOREST CUPCAKES

INSPIRED BY MY GERMAN ORIGINS, I HAVE TWEAKED THE CLASSIC BLACK FOREST GATEAÛX AND TURNED IT INTO A SUMPTUOUS CUPCAKE RECIPE. THE KEY IS TO USE PROPER 'GRIOTTINES' CHERRIES, WHICH ARE WILD MORELLO CHERRIES, SOAKED IN KIRSCH LIQUEUR. THEY TASTE HEAVENLY – PLUMP, JUICY AND VERY BOOZEY.

Makes approximately 24 cupcakes

ingredients

For the decoration
About 150g white sugar florist paste
Pink and brown paste food colour
Small amount of royal icing (see pages 182–3)
Small amount of white vegetable fat

For the frosting
200g full-fat cream cheese
200g unsalted butter
500g icing sugar, sifted
Small amount of Kirsch syrup, drained
from the cherries (see below)

For the cake mix
125g plain chocolate (minimum 53%
cocoa solids), chopped or buttons
165ml milk
285g light brown sugar
105g unsalted butter, softened
2 large eggs
180g plain flour
Pinch of salt
½ tsp baking powder
½ tsp bicarbonate of soda
8g cocoa powder
350g Griottine cherries in Kirsch syrup

For the sugar syrup
150ml water
150g caster sugar
Small amount of Kirsch syrup, drained
from the cherries (see above)
50ml Kirsch liqueur

equipment

Basic baking kit (see page 172)
Small non-stick plastic board
Medium and small five-petal blossom cutter
Blossom veiner
Paint palette or perforated foam,
to dry blossoms
Paper piping bag (see page 184)
Two 12-hole muffin trays
24 large brown cupcake cases
Plastic piping bags
Large star piping nozzle

To make the decoration
Following the instructions on page 174, make the sugar cherry blossom decorations at least one day ahead of assembling and serving. Make two or three blossoms per cupcake.

Mix the sugar florist paste with a small amount of pink paste food colour to make a fuchsia shade. Mix the royal icing with the brown paste food colour following the instructions on pages 182–3. Using a blossom cutter and

veiner, make approximately 72 sugar blossoms then pipe a brown centre into each flower. Leave to dry.

Preheat the oven to 175°C/gas mark 4. Prepare the muffin trays by placing the cupcake cases inside the holes.

To make the frosting
Place the cream cheese in a mixing bowl and beat until smooth and creamy.

USING A STAR-SHAPED NOZZLE, PIPE SWIRLS OF FROSTING OVER THE TOPS OF EACH CUPCAKE ENDING WITH A PERFECT PEAK.

Place the butter and icing sugar in a separate mixing bowl and cream together until very pale and fluffy.

Add the cream cheese, a little at a time, to the butter mixture and mix at medium-high speed until the frosting is combined.

Flavour to taste with a few drops of the Kirsch syrup, making sure the frosting doesn't become too runny. Chill until set.

To make the cupcakes

Place the chocolate, milk and half the sugar into a saucepan. Gently bring to the boil whilst stirring.

Place the butter and remaining sugar in a mixing bowl and cream together until very pale and fluffy.

Beat the eggs lightly in another bowl and slowly stir into the butter mixture.

Sift the flour, baking powder, bicarbonate of soda and cocoa powder into the batter and mix until just combined.

Slowly pour the hot chocolate into the batter and mix. Scrape the bowl with a rubber spatula to make sure the batter is well combined. Transfer the batter to a measuring jug.

While still warm. pour the batter into the cupcake cases until two-thirds full only. Drop 2 or 3 griottine cherries into each cupcake.

Bake immediately for 15–20 minutes, depending on your oven. The cupcakes are cooked when the tops spring back to the touch. If you insert a clean knife or wooden skewer into the centre of the sponge, it should come out with a small amount of crumb sticking to it.

To make the sugar syrup

While the cupcakes are baking, prepare the sugar syrup for soaking. Place the water and caster sugar into a saucepan and bring to the boil. Simmer until all the sugar crystals have dissolved. Set aside to cool down slightly. Flavour with some of the Kirsch syrup and Kirsch liqueur.

As soon as the cupcakes are baked, take them out of the oven. Using a pastry brush, soak the tops of the cupcakes with sugar syrup while they are still hot; this allows the syrup to be absorbed faster and prevent it from forming a crusty top.

Remove the cupcakes from the baking trays and leave to cool completely on a wire cooling rack.

To decorate

Following the instructions on page 178, prepare a plastic piping bag fitted with a large star nozzle. Fill with the chilled frosting. Pipe a rosette of frosting on top of each cupcake.

To finish, place 2 or 3 sugar blossoms on the top of the frosting for each cupcake.

STRAWBERRY AND CHAMPAGNE CUPCAKES

A SOPHISTICATED AND DELECTABLE CUPCAKE RECIPE,
PERFECT FOR A GARDEN PARTY IN THE BRITISH SUMMER.
ENJOY WITH A GLASS OF PINK CHAMPAGNE.

Makes approximately 24 cupcakes

ingredients

For the frosting
200g full-fat cream cheese
200g unsalted butter, softened
500g icing sugar, sifted
Marc de Champagne, to taste
Pink paste food colour

For the cake mix
200g unsalted butter, softened
200g caster sugar
Pinch of salt
Seeds of 1 vanilla pod
4 medium eggs
200g self-raising flour

For the syrup
150ml water
150g caster sugar
Marc de Champagne, to taste

For the filling
About 350g Peggy's Strawberry
& Champagne Jam or any
other good-quality strawberry jam

For the decoration
12 small strawberries

equipment

Basic baking kit (see page 172)
Two 12-hole muffin trays
24 large silver cupcake cases
Plastic piping bags
Large star piping nozzle

Preheat the oven to 175°C/gas mark 4. Prepare the muffin trays by placing the cupcake cases inside the holes.

To make the frosting
Place the cream cheese in a mixing bowl and beat until smooth and creamy.

Place the butter and icing sugar in a separate mixing bowl and cream together until very pale and fluffy.

Add the cream cheese, a little at a time, to the butter mixture and mix at medium-high speed until the frosting is combined.

Flavour to taste with the Marc de Champagne, making sure the frosting doesn't become too runny. Add a small amount of pink paste food colour and mix to a pale pastel shade. Chill until set.

To make the cupcakes
Place the butter, sugar, salt and vanilla seeds in a mixing bowl and cream together until pale and fluffy.

Beat the eggs lightly in another bowl and slowly pour into the butter mixture while whisking quickly. If the mixture starts to separate or curdle, stop adding the egg and beat in 2–3 tablespoons of flour. This will rebind the batter.

Once all the egg has been incorporated into the butter mixture, sift in the flour and stir until the batter is just combined. This will ensure the sponges stay light and fluffy.

Using a plastic piping bag or a tablespoon, carefully place the batter into the cupcake cases until two-thirds full only.

Bake for 12–15 minutes, depending on your oven. The cupcakes are cooked when the tops are golden brown and spring back to the touch. If in doubt, insert a clean knife or wooden skewer into the centre of each sponge; it should come out clean.

To make the sugar syrup
While the cupcakes are baking, prepare the sugar syrup for soaking. Place the water and caster sugar into a saucepan and bring to the boil. Simmer until all the sugar crystals have dissolved. Set aside to cool. Once cool, flavour to taste with the Marc de Champagne.

Once the cupcakes are baked, let them rest for about 10 minutes outside of the oven. Using a pastry brush, soak the tops of the cupcakes with sugar syrup while they are still warm; this allows the syrup to be absorbed faster.

Once just warm, remove the cupcakes from the baking trays and leave to cool completely on a wire cooling rack.

Once cool, wrap the cupcakes in cling film and then chill for 1 hour or until the sponge feels firm to the touch. Using a melon baller, scoop out the tops of each cupcake.

To add the filling
Using a teaspoon, fill the scooped-out holes of the cupcakes with the strawberry jam.

To decorate
Wash and cut the strawberries in half.

Following the instructions on page 178, prepare a plastic piping bag fitted with a star nozzle. Fill with the chilled frosting. Pipe a rosette of frosting on top of each cupcake.

To finish, place a strawberry half on the top of the frosting for each cupcake.

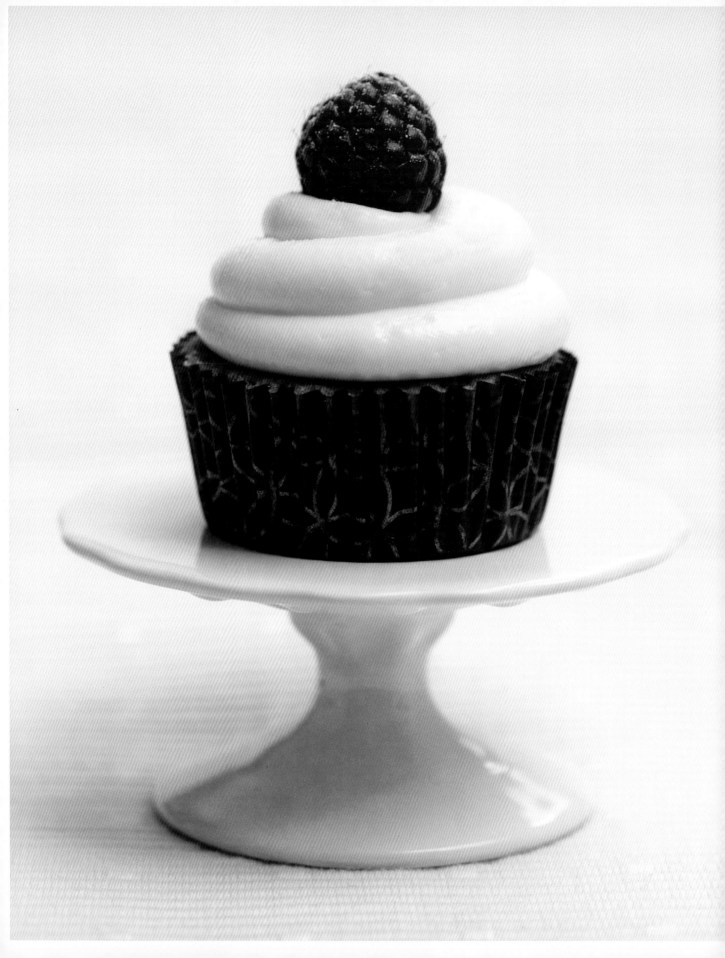

LEMON AND RASPBERRY CUPCAKES

THIS IS A VERY SIMPLE AND LIGHT CUPCAKE THAT TASTES REFRESHING ON A SUMMER'S DAY. THE COMBINATION OF LEMON AND RASPBERRY CREATES A PERFECT BALANCE AND CUTS THROUGH THE SWEET CREAM CHEESE FROSTING.

Makes approximately 24 cupcakes

ingredients

For the frosting
200g full-fat cream cheese
200g unsalted butter, softened
500g icing sugar, sifted
Finely grated zest of 2 unwaxed lemons

For the sponge
200g unsalted butter, softened
200g caster sugar
Pinch of salt
Finely grated zest of 2 lemons
4 medium eggs
200g self-raising flour
Punnet of raspberries, plus extra for
the decoration

For the sugar syrup
150ml freshly squeezed lemon juice
150g caster sugar

equipment

Basic baking kit (see page 172)
Two 12-hole muffin trays
24 large brown cupcake cases
Plastic piping bags
Large round piping nozzle

Preheat the oven to 175°C/gas mark 4. Prepare the muffin trays by placing the cupcake cases inside the holes.

To make the frosting
Place the cream cheese in a mixing bowl and beat until smooth and creamy. Place the butter, icing sugar and lemon zest in a separate bowl and cream together until very pale and fluffy. Add the cream cheese, a little at a time, to the butter mixture and mix at medium-high speed until the frosting is combined. Chill until set.

To make the cupcakes
Place the butter, sugar, salt and lemon zest in a mixing bowl and cream together until pale and fluffy. Beat the eggs lightly in another bowl and slowly pour into the butter mixture while whisking quickly. If the mixture starts to separate or curdle, stop adding the egg and beat in 2–3 tablespoons of the flour. This will rebind the batter. Once all the egg has been incorporated into the butter mixture, sift in the flour and stir until the batter is just combined. This ensures the sponges stay light and fluffy.

Using a piping bag or tablespoon, place the batter into the cupcake cases until two-thirds full. Drop 2 or 3 raspberries into each cupcake.

Bake for 12–15 minutes, depending on your oven. The cupcakes are cooked when the tops are golden brown and spring back to the touch. If in doubt, insert a clean knife or wooden skewer into the centre of each sponge; it should come out clean.

To make the sugar syrup
While the cupcakes are baking, prepare the sugar syrup for soaking. Place the lemon juice and caster sugar into a saucepan and bring to the boil. Simmer until all the sugar crystals have dissolved. Set aside to cool down slightly.

Once the cupcakes are baked, let them rest for about 10 minutes outside of the oven. Using a pastry brush, soak the tops of the cupcakes with sugar syrup while they are still warm; this allows the syrup to be absorbed faster. Once warm, remove the cupcakes from the trays and leave to cool on a wire cooling rack.

To decorate
Following the instructions on page 178, prepare a plastic piping bag fitted with a large round nozzle. Fill with the chilled frosting. Pipe a swirl of frosting on top of each cupcake. To finish, place a raspberry on the top of the frosting for each cupcake.

VANILLA CHIFFON CUPCAKES

THIS IS A VERY LIGHT AND FLUFFY RECIPE USING REAL VANILLA AND CREAM CHEESE FROSTING. THE BEAUTY IS IN ITS SIMPLICITY AND PURITY OF FLAVOURS. LESS IS SOMETIMES MORE...

Makes approximately 24 cupcakes

ingredients

For the decoration
50g white sugar florist paste
Small amount of white vegetable fat
Small amount of royal icing (see pages 182–3)
Yellow paste food colour

For the frosting
200g full-fat cream cheese
200g unsalted butter, softened
500g icing sugar, sifted
Seeds of ½ vanilla pod
Yellow, orange and teal paste food colour

For the sponge
200g unsalted butter, softened
200g caster sugar
Pinch of salt
Seeds of ½ vanilla pod
4 medium eggs
200g self-raising flour

For the sugar syrup
150ml water
150g caster sugar
Scraped vanilla pod

equipment

Basic baking kit (see page 172)
Small non-stick plastic board
Small five-petal blossom cutter and veiner
Paint palette or perforated foam pad,
to dry blossoms
Paper piping bag (see page 184)
Two 12-hole muffin trays
24 large brown cupcake cases

To make the decoration
Following the instructions on page 174, make the sugar blossom decorations one day ahead of assembling and serving. Make one blossom per cupcake.

Mix the sugar florist paste with a small amount of vegetable fat. Mix the royal icing with the yellow paste food colour following the instructions on pages 182–3. Using a blossom cutter and veiner, make 24 sugar blossoms then pipe a yellow centre into each flower. Leave to dry.

Preheat the oven to 175°C/gas mark 4. Prepare the muffin trays by placing the cupcake cases inside the holes.

To make the frosting
Place the cream cheese in a mixing bowl and beat until smooth and creamy.

USING A SMALL PALETTE KNIFE, PILE THE FROSTING ONTO THE TOPS OF
EACH CUPCAKE AND THEN SMOOTH OVER .

Place the butter, icing sugar and vanilla seeds in a separate mixing bowl and cream together until very pale and fluffy.

Add the cream cheese, a little at a time, to the butter mixture and mix at medium-high speed until the frosting is combined. Chill until set.

To make the cupcakes
Place the butter, sugar, salt and vanilla seeds in a mixing bowl and cream together until pale and fluffy.

Beat the eggs lightly in another bowl and slowly add to the butter mixture while whisking quickly. If the mixture starts to separate or curdle, stop adding the egg and beat in 2–3 tablespoons of flour. This will rebind the batter.

Once all the egg has been incorporated into the butter mixture, sift in the flour and stir until the batter is just combined. This will ensure the sponges stay light and fluffy.

Using a plastic piping bag or a tablespoon, carefully place the batter into the cupcake cases until two-thirds full only.

Bake for 12–15 minutes, depending on your oven. The cupcakes are cooked when the tops are golden brown and spring back to the touch. If in doubt, insert a clean knife or wooden skewer into the centre of each sponge; it should come out clean.

To make the sugar syrup
While the cupcakes are baking, prepare the sugar syrup for soaking. Place the water, sugar and vanilla pod into a saucepan and bring to the boil. Simmer until all the sugar crystals have dissolved. Set aside to cool down slightly. Discard the vanilla pod.

Once the cupcakes are baked, let them rest for about 10 minutes outside of the oven. Using a pastry brush, soak the tops of the cupcakes with sugar syrup while they are still warm; this allows the syrup to be absorbed faster.

Once just warm, remove the cupcakes from the trays and leave to cool completely on a wire cooling rack.

To decorate
Divide the frosting into three equal parts. Mix the first third with a small amount of yellow paste food colour, the second with orange paste food colour and the third with teal paste food colour.

Following the instructions on page 179, frost the cupcakes using a small palette knife.

To finish, place a sugar blossom on the top of the frosting for each cupcake.

CHOCOLATE HEAVEN CUPCAKES

THIS CUPCAKE TASTES REALLY HEAVENLY. IT IS RICH, CREAMY
AND SMOOTH, YET NOT TOO HEAVY. MOST OF ALL, IT IS VERY CHOCOLATEY.
THIS RECIPE IS SO YUMMY, WE HAVE EVEN WON AN AWARD FOR IT!

Makes approximately 24 cupcakes

ingredients

For the frosting
140ml whipping cream
160g plain chocolate (minimum 53%
cocoa solids), chopped or in buttons
1 tbsp glucose
200g full-fat cream cheese
200g salted butter, softened
450g icing sugar, sifted

For the cake mix
125g plain chocolate (minimum 53%
cocoa solids), chopped or buttons
165ml milk
285g light brown sugar
105g unsalted butter, softened
2 large eggs
180g plain flour
Pinch of salt
½ tsp baking powder
½ tsp bicarbonate of soda
8g cocoa powder

For the decoration
Sheets of rice paper
Edible lustre spray in pearlised
pink, blue and green

equipment

Basic baking kit (see page 172)
Two 12-hole muffin trays
24 large brown cupcake cases
Plastic piping bag
Large star piping nozzle
24 pearlised scallop-edged cupcake wrappers
Flower paper punch
(available from craft shops)

To make the decoration
Following the instructions on page 175, make the rice paper blossom decorations. Make one rice paper blossom per cupcake.

Preheat the oven to 160°C/gas mark 3. Prepare the muffin trays by placing the cupcake cases inside the holes.

To make the frosting
Place the cream in a saucepan and bring to a bare simmer. Place the chocolate and glucose into a bowl and pour the hot cream over the top. Whisk together until smooth, shiny and all the chocolate has melted. Once combined, leave to set at room temperature; the ganache should have the consistency of soft butter.

Place the cream cheese in a mixing bowl and beat until smooth and creamy.

Place the butter and icing sugar in a separate mixing bowl and cream together until very pale and fluffy.

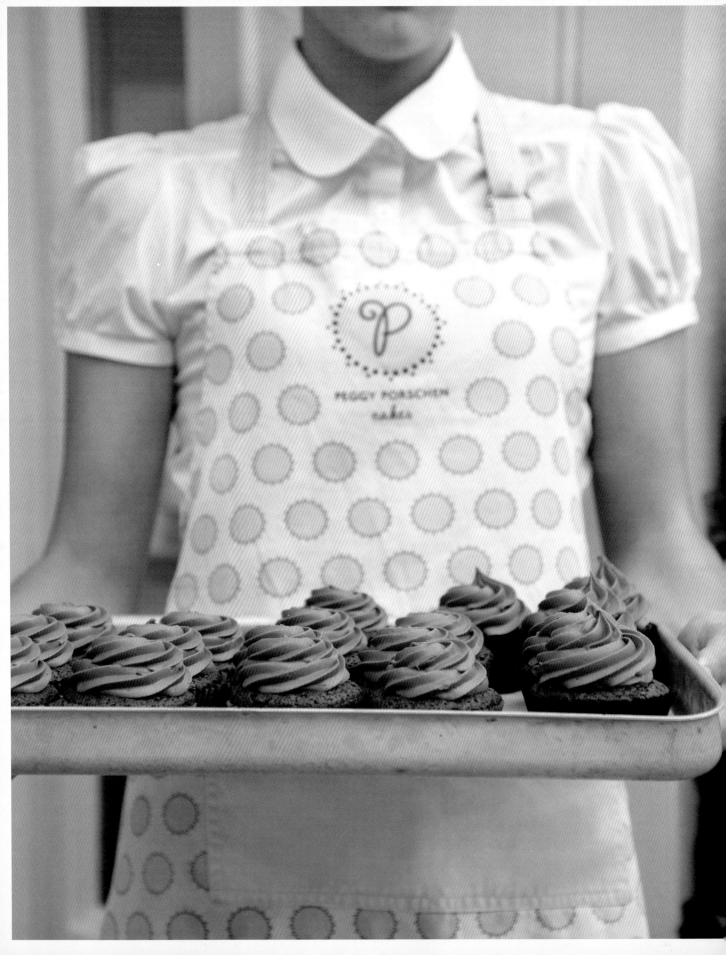

Add the ganache, a little at a time, to the buttercream mixture and mix at medium-high speed until the frosting is combined.

Gently stir one-third of the chocolate buttercream into the cream cheese.

Slowly whisk the remaining buttercream and add the chocolate cream cheese in two batches. Take care not to overwork the frosting as it can split. Chill until set.

To make the cupcakes
Place the chocolate, milk and half the sugar into a saucepan. Gently bring to the boil whilst stirring.

Place the butter and remaining sugar in a mixing bowl and cream together until very pale and fluffy.

Beat the eggs lightly in another bowl and slowly stir into the butter mixture.

Sift the flour, baking powder, bicarbonate of soda, salt and cocoa powder together and add to the batter in two batches. Slowly mix until just combined.

Slowly pour the hot chocolate into the batter and mix. Scrape the bowl with a rubber spatula to make sure the batter is well combined. Transfer the batter to a measuring jug.

While still warm, pour the batter into the cupcake cases until two-thirds full only.

Bake immediately for 12–15 minutes, depending on your oven. The cupcakes are cooked when tops spring back to the touch and the edges have shrunk away from the side. Once cooked, the texture of this sponge is slightly sticky and dense. If you insert a clean knife or wooden skewer into the centre of the sponge, it should come out with a small amount of crumb sticking to it.

Once the cupcakes are baked let them rest for a few minutes outside of the oven. Once just warm, remove the cupcakes from the baking trays and leave to cool completely on a wire cooling rack.

To decorate
Following the instructions on page 178, prepare a plastic piping bag fitted with a large star nozzle. Fill with the chilled frosting Pipe a rosette of frosting on top of each cupcake.

To finish, place each cupcake into a wrapper and press a rice paper blossom on the top of the frosting for each cupcake.

COSMO CUPCAKES

CUPCAKES AND COCKTAILS GO HAND IN HAND, AND THE COSMOPOLITAN LENDS ITSELF PERFECTLY AS INSPIRATION FOR THIS RECIPE. FOR PARTY FUN, SERVE IN COCKTAIL GLASSES OR STICK SHORT DRINKING STRAWS INTO THE ICING.

Makes approximately 24 cupcakes

ingredients

For the sponge
125g dried cranberries
Cointreau™ liqueur, for soaking
200g unsalted butter, softened
200g caster sugar
Pinch of salt
Finely grated zest of 2 oranges
4 medium eggs
200g self-raising flour
For the frosting
200g full-fat cream cheese
200g unsalted butter, softened
Pinch of salt
500g icing sugar, sifted

Finely grated zest of 2 oranges
A dash of Cointreau liqueur, to taste
For the sugar syrup
150ml freshly squeezed orange juice
150g caster sugar
50ml Cointreau liqueur
For the decoration
Metallic pink sugar pearls

equipment

Basic baking kit (see page 172)
Plastic piping bag
Two 12-hole muffin trays
24 large metallic pink cupcake cases
Large star piping nozzle

Soak the cranberries in Cointreau™ liqueur, cover with clingfilm and leave to infuse overnight.

Preheat the oven to 175°C/gas mark 4. Prepare the muffin trays by placing the cupcake cases inside the holes.

To make the frosting
Following the instructions given on page 73, make the frosting using orange zest. Flavour with Cointreau™ liqueur to taste. Chill until set.

To make the cupcakes
Place the butter, sugar, salt and orange zest in a mixing bowl and cream together until pale and fluffy. Beat the eggs lightly in another bowl and slowly add to the butter mixture while whisking quickly. If the mixture starts to separate or curdle, stop adding the egg and beat in 2–3 tablespoons of flour. This will rebind the batter. Once all the egg has been incorporated into the butter mixture, sift in the flour and stir until the batter is just combined. This will ensure the sponges stay light and fluffy.

Using a piping bag or tablespoon, place the batter into the cupcake cases until two-thirds full only. Drain the cranberries, reserving the liquid to add to the sugar syrup. Divide the cranberries evenly and drop into the cupcakes.

Bake for 12–15 minutes, depending on your oven. The cupcakes are cooked when the tops are golden brown and spring back to the touch. If in doubt, insert a clean knife or wooden skewer into the centre of each sponge; it should come out clean.

To make the sugar syrup
While the cupcakes are baking, prepare the sugar syrup for soaking. Place the orange juice and caster sugar into a saucepan and bring to the boil. Simmer until all the sugar crystals have dissolved. Set aside to cool slightly. Flavour with the reserved Cointreau™ liquid to taste.

Once the cupcakes are baked, let them rest for 10 minutes outside of the oven. Using a pastry brush, soak the tops of the cupcakes with sugar syrup while they are still warm; this allows the syrup to be absorbed faster. Once warm, remove the cupcakes from the trays and leave to cool on a wire cooling rack.

To decorate
Following the instructions on page 178, prepare a plastic piping bag fitted with a large star nozzle. Fill with the chilled frosting. Pipe a rosette of frosting on top of each cupcake. To finish, sprinkle pink sugar pearls over the frosting for each cupcake.

LUSCIOUS
LAYER CAKES

SUMMER BERRY CAKE

AN UTTERLY SCRUMPTIOUS RECIPE FOR THE SERIOUSLY SWEET-TOOTHED
COMBINING HEAVENLY LIGHT BUTTERCREAM,
FLUFFY VANILLA SPONGE AND SWEET SUMMER BERRIES.
Makes one 15cm (6in) round cake, serving 8–12 slices

ingredients

For the sponge
200g unsalted butter, softened
200g caster sugar
Pinch of salt
Seeds of 1 vanilla pod
4 medium eggs
200g self-raising flour
For the sugar syrup
150ml water
150g caster sugar
Scraped vanilla pod
For the buttercream filling
250g unsalted butter, softened
250g icing sugar, sifted
Pinch of salt
3 tbsp Peggy's Summer Berry Jam or
any other good-quality mixed berry jam
For the decoration
1 tbsp cocoa powder

equipment

Basic baking kit (see page 172)
Three 15cm (6in) round sandwich tins
Cake leveller or large serrated knife
Non-slip turntable
Flat disc to place on top of the turntable
(I use the loose base of a 30cm (12in)
springform cake tin)
Metal side scraper
Laser-cut damask cake stencil

Bake the sponges one day ahead of serving. Make the sugar syrup whilst baking the sponges. Prepare the buttercream filling and assemble and decorate the cake on the day of serving. Dust the cake with the cocoa powder immediately before serving as, after a few hours, the cocoa powder may absorb moisture from the buttercream and appear wet.

Preheat the oven to 175°C/gas mark 4.

Prepare the sandwich tins by greasing the sides and lining the bases with greaseproof paper. Place the tin on top of the greaseproof paper, draw a line around the base with a pencil and use that as a guide to cut out a disc to line the base. Place the greasproof paper discs inside the tins.

To make the sponge
Place the butter, sugar, salt and vanilla seeds into a mixing bowl and cream together until pale and fluffy.

Beat the eggs lightly in another bowl and slowly add to the butter mixture while whisking quickly. If the mixture starts to separate or curdle, stop adding the egg and beat in 2–3 tablespoons of the flour. This will rebind the batter. Once all the egg has been added and combined with the butter mixture, sift in the flour and fold through until the batter is just combined. This will ensure the sponges stay light and fluffy.

Divide the batter evenly between the cake tins. If you find it difficult to measure by eye, use your kitchen scales to weigh out the amount of sponge mixture for each tin.

Bake for 15–20 minutes, depending on your oven. If you are using deeper cake tins, the

TO DECORATE, CENTRE THE STENCIL ON TOP OF THE CAKE AND DUST THE SURFACE WITH COCOA POWDER. LIFT THE STENCIL OFF THE CAKE.

sponges may take longer to cook. The sponges are cooked when the sides are beginning to shrink away from the edges of the tins and the tops are golden brown and spring back to the touch. If in doubt, insert a clean knife or wooden skewer into the centre of each sponge; it should come out clean.

To make the sugar syrup

While the sponges are baking, prepare the sugar syrup for soaking. Place the water, caster sugar and vanilla pod into a saucepan and bring to the boil. Simmer until all the sugar crystals have dissolved. Set aside to cool down slightly.

Once the sponges are baked, let them rest for about 10 minutes outside of the oven. Using a pastry brush, soak the tops of the sponges with syrup while they are still warm; this allows the syrup to be absorbed faster.

Once just warm, run a knife all the way round the sides of the tins, then remove the sponges from the tins and leave to cool completely on a wire cooling rack.

Once cool, wrap the sponges in cling film and then rest them overnight at room temperature. This will ensure that all the moisture is sealed in and the sponges firm up to the perfect texture for trimming and layering. When trimmed

too soon after baking, the sponges tend to crumble and may even break into pieces.

To make the buttercream filling

Place the butter, icing sugar and salt into a mixing bowl and cream together until very pale and fluffy.

Add the jam to the mixture and stir through until combined. If the jam is a little too firm or chunky to mix easily, warm it up in a microwave or pass it through a coarse sieve to remove any larger berries. Alternatively, blitz the jam in a blender.

To assemble the cake

Trim and sandwich together the three sponge layers using one-third of the buttercream filling. With the remaining buttercream filling, cover and mask the top and sides of the cake. For full instructions on how to do this, see pages 180–81.

To decorate

Centre the damask cake stencil on the top of the masked cake. Dust the surface liberally with cocoa powder. Carefully lift the stencil off the cake to reveal the damask pattern.

Serve the cake at room temperature. This cake is best enjoyed within 3 days of baking, but it can last for up to 1 week

tip

When making the sponges, use three shallow sandwich tins rather than one deep cake tin as the sponges will rise better and bake more evenly.

TIPSY ORANGE TRUFFLE CAKE

DELICIOUSLY FRAGRANT ORANGE SPONGE INFUSED WITH COINTREAU
AND LAYERED WITH BITTERSWEET DARK CHOCOLATE GANACHE,
THIS PARLOUR FAVOURITE IS THE ULTIMATE CHOCOLATE ORANGE RECIPE.
A VERY GROWN-UP, SERIOUSLY SMOOTH AND YUMMY CAKE!

Makes one 15cm (6in) round cake, serving 8-12 slices

ingredients

For the sponge
200g unsalted butter, softened
200g caster sugar
Pinch of salt
Finely grated zest of 3 oranges
4 medium eggs
200g self-raising flour

For the sugar syrup
Juice of 3 freshly squeezed oranges
150g caster sugar
2 tbsp Cointreau™ orange liqueur

For the ganache
250ml whipping cream
300g plain chocolate (minimum 53%
cocoa solids), chopped or in buttons
1 tsp glucose

For the filling
2 tbsp Peggy's Orange & Cointreau™
Marmalade or any other good-quality
orange marmalade

equipment

Basic baking kit (see page 172)
Three 15cm (6in) round sandwich tins
Large serrated knife or cake leveller
Non-slip turntable
Flat disc to place on top of the turntable
(I use the loose base of a 30cm (12in)
springform cake tin)
Metal side scraper
Paper piping bag

Bake the sponges one day ahead of serving Make the sugar syrup whilst baking the sponges. Prepare the filling and assemble and decorate the cake on the day of serving.

Preheat the oven to 175°C/gas mark 4.

Prepare the sandwich tins by greasing and lining them with greaseproof paper. For full instructions on how to do this, see page 87.

To make the sponge
Place the butter, sugar, salt and orange zest into a mixing bowl and cream together until pale and fluffy.

Beat the eggs lightly in another bowl and slowly add to the butter mixture while whisking quickly. If the mixture starts to separate or curdle, stop adding the egg and beat in 2–3 tablespoons of the flour. This will rebind the batter. Once all the egg has been added and combined with the butter mixture, sift in the flour and stir until the batter is just combined. This will ensure the sponges stay light and fluffy.

Divide the batter evenly between the cake tins. If you find it difficult to measure by eye, use your kitchen scales to weigh out the amount of sponge mixture for each tin.

Bake for 15–20 minutes, depending on your oven. If you are using deeper cake tins, the sponges will take longer to cook. The sponges are cooked when the sides are beginning to shrink away from the edges of the tins and the tops are golden brown and spring back to the touch. If in doubt, insert a clean knife or wooden skewer into the centre of each sponge; it should come out clean.

To make the sugar syrup
While the sponges are baking, prepare the sugar syrup for soaking. Place the orange juice and caster sugar into a saucepan and bring to the boil. Simmer until all the sugar crystals have dissolved. Set aside to cool down slightly and then add the orange liqueur.

Once the sponges are baked, let them rest for about 10 minutes outside of the oven. Using a pastry brush, soak the tops of the sponges with syrup while they are still warm; this allows the syrup to be absorbed faster.

Once just warm, run a knife all the way round the sides of the tins, remove the sponges from the tins and leave to cool completely on a wire cooling rack.

Once cool, wrap the sponges in cling film and then rest them overnight at room temperature. This will ensure that all the moisture is sealed in and the sponges firm up to the perfect texture for trimming and layering. When trimmed too soon after baking, the sponges tend to crumble and may even break into pieces.

To make the ganache
Place the cream in a saucepan and bring to a simmer. Place the chocolate in a bowl and pour over the hot cream. Gently stir with a whisk or spatula until the chocolate has melted. Add the glucose and allow the ganache to set until it has a butter-like consistency.

To assemble the cake
Trim and sandwich together the three sponge layers using 2 tablespoons of ganache for the first layer and 2 tablespoons of marmalade for the second layer. Using half of the remaining ganache, cover or crumb-coat the top and sides of the cake. For full instructions on how to do this, see pages 180–81.

To glaze the cake
Place the cake on a wire cooling rack and slide a tray underneath. Reserve approximately 1 tablespoon of the ganache for piping the decoration, then warm the remaining ganache to a thick pouring consistency. Pour the warmed ganache over the top of the cake ensuring the sides are evenly covered. Tap the tray to spread out the ganache and pop any air bubbles that appear. Chill the cake until set.

To decorate
Place the cake on top of the turntable. Fill a paper piping bag with the reserved ganache, snip a small hole from the tip of the bag and pipe a swag border around the circumference of the cake top, revolving the turntable as necessary.

Serve the cake at room temperature. This cake is best enjoyed within 3 days of baking, but it can last for up to 1 week

LEMON LIMONCELLO CAKE

THIS IS A VERY LOVELY CAKE – LIGHT, MOIST AND FULL OF FLAVOUR.
A SCATTERING OF CUTE SUGAR DAISIES COMPLEMENTS THE REFRESHING
PALE LEMON BUTTERCREAM ICING.
Makes one 15cm (6in) round cake, serving 8-12 slices

ingredients

For the decoration
150g white sugar florist paste
Small amount of white vegetable fat
Green and yellow paste food colour
Small amount of royal icing (see pages 182–3)

For the sponge
200g unsalted butter, softened
200g caster sugar
Pinch of salt
Finely grated zest of 2 unwaxed lemons
4 medium eggs
200g self-raising flour

For the sugar syrup
150ml freshly squeezed lemon juice
150g caster sugar
50ml Limoncello liqueur

For the buttercream filling
80g unsalted butter
80g icing sugar, sifted
Pinch of salt
40g Peggy's Lemon Limoncello Jelly or any
other good-quality lemon jelly or lemon curd

equipment

Basic baking kit (see page 172)
Three 15cm (6in) round sandwich tins
Cake leveller or large serrated knife
Non-slip turntable
Flat disc to place on top of the turntable
(I use the loose base of a 30cm (12in)
springform cake tin)
15cm (6in) round cake card
Metal side scraper
For the sugar daisies and leaves,
see the equipment list on page 173

Following the instructions on page 173, make the simple daisies and leaves decoration at least one day ahead of assembling and serving. Bake the sponges one day ahead of serving. Make the sugar syrup whilst baking the sponges. Prepare the filling and assemble and decorate the cake on the day of serving.

To make the decoration
Mix two thirds of the sugar florist paste with a small amount of white vegetable fat. Mix the remaining third with the green paste food colour to a pale green shade. Mix the royal icing with the yellow paste food colour to a pale lemon shade following the instructions

on page 182–3. Using a daisy plunge cutter, leaf cutter and veiner, make approximately 12 simple sugar daisies and small leaves. Leave to set in a cool dry place.

Preheat the oven to 175°C/gas mark 4.

Prepare the sandwich tins by greasing and lining them with greaseproof paper. For full instructions on how to do this, see page 87.

To make the sponge
Place the butter, sugar, salt and lemon zest into a mixing bowl and cream together until pale and fluffy.

Beat the eggs lightly in another bowl and slowly add to the butter mixture while whisking quickly. If the mixture starts to separate or curdle, stop adding the egg and beat in 2–3 tablespoons of the flour. This will rebind the batter. Once all the egg has been added and combined with the butter mixture, sift in the flour and stir until the batter is just combined. This will ensure the sponges stay light and fluffy.

Divide the batter evenly between the sandwich tins. If you find it difficult to measure by eye, use your kitchen scales to weigh out the amount of sponge mixture for each tin.

Bake for 15–20 minutes, depending on your oven. If you are using deeper cake tins, the sponges will take longer to cook. The sponges are cooked when the sides are beginning to shrink away from the edges of the tins and the tops are golden brown and spring back to the touch. If in doubt, insert a clean knife or wooden skewer into the centre of each sponge; it should come out clean.

To make the sugar syrup
While the sponges are baking, prepare the sugar syrup for soaking. Place the lemon juice and caster sugar in a saucepan and bring to the boil. Simmer until all the sugar crystals have dissolved. Set aside to cool down slightly and then add the Limoncello liqueur.

Once the sponges are baked, let them rest for about 10 minutes outside of the oven. Using a pastry brush, soak the tops of the sponges with syrup while they are still warm; this allows the syrup to be absorbed faster.

Once just warm, run a knife all the way round the sides of the tins, remove the sponges from the tins and leave to cool completely on a wire cooling rack.

Once cool, wrap the sponges in cling film and then rest them overnight at room temperature. This will ensure that all the moisture is sealed in and the sponges firm up to the perfect texture for trimming and layering. When trimmed too soon after baking, the sponges tend to crumble and may even break into pieces.

To make the buttercream filling
Place the butter, icing sugar and salt into a mixing bowl and cream together until very pale and fluffy. Add the lemon jelly to the mixture and stir through until combined and smooth.

To assemble the cake
Trim and sandwich together the three sponge layers using one-third of the buttercream filling and the limoncello syrup for soaking. With the remaining buttercream filling, cover or mask the top and sides of the cake. For full instructions on how to do this, see pages 180–81. Chill until set.

To decorate
Arrange the sugar daisies and leaves around the circumference of the cake top and stick them down with a dab of buttercream.

Serve the cake at room temperature. This cake is best enjoyed within 3 days of baking, but it can last for up to 1 week

tip

Decorations made from sugar can attract moisture and may collapse when exposed to humid conditions. Therefore, do not store the cake in the fridge once decorated if it is not being eaten on the same day.

CREAMY CARAMEL CAKE

A SUMPTUOUS RECIPE FOR LOVERS OF ALL THINGS SWEET. THE HINT OF BRANDY PERFECTLY COMPLEMENTS THE CARAMEL FLAVOURS WHILE THE SCULPTED DESIGN AND COCOA DUSTING CREATE A COOL CONTEMPORARY LOOK.

Makes one 15cm (6in) round cake, serving 8-12 slices

ingredients

For the sponge
200g unsalted butter, softened
200g caster sugar
Pinch of salt
Seeds of 1 vanilla pod
4 medium eggs
200g self-raising flour

For the sugar syrup
150ml water
150g caster sugar
scraped vanilla pod
2 tbsp Brandy

For the buttercream filling
100g unsalted butter
100g icing sugar, sifted
Pinch of salt
50g dulce de leche or a can of sweetened condensed milk boiled in water for 3 hours

For the decoration
About 2 tbsp cocoa powder

equipment

Basic baking kit (see page 172)
Three 15cm (6in) round sandwich tins
Cake leveller or large serrated knife
Non-slip turntable
Flat disc to place on top of the turntable
(I use the loose base of a 30cm (12in) springform cake tin)
15cm (6in) round cake card
Ridged side scraper (I use one from Wilton)

Bake the sponges one day ahead of serving. Make the sugar syrup whilst baking the sponges. Prepare the filling and assemble and decorate the cake on the day of serving. Dust the cake with the cocoa powder immediately before serving as, after a few hours, the cocoa powder may absorb moisture from the buttercream and appear wet.

Preheat the oven to 175°C/gas mark 4.

Prepare the sandwich tins by greasing and lining them with greaseproof paper. For full instructions on how to do this, see page 87.

To make the sponge
Place the butter, sugar, salt and vanilla seeds in a mixing bowl and cream together until pale and fluffy.

Beat the eggs lightly in another bowl and slowly add to the butter mixture while whisking quickly. If the mixture starts to separate or curdle, stop adding the egg and beat in 2-3 tablespoons of flour. This will rebind the batter. Once all the egg has been added and combined with the butter mixture, sift in the flour and stir until the batter is just combined. This will ensure the sponges stay light and fluffy.

Divide the batter evenly between the cake tins. If you find it difficult to measure by eye, use your kitchen scales to weigh out the amount of sponge mixture for each tin.

Bake for 15-20 minutes, depending on your oven. If you are using deeper cake tins, the sponges will take longer to cook. The sponges are cooked when the sides are beginning to

USE A RIDGED SIDE SCRAPER TO CREATE THE SCULPTED BARREL DESIGN AROUND THE CAKE. SMOOTH OVER THE TOP WITH A PALETTE KNIFE.

shrink away from the edges of the tins and the tops are golden brown and spring back to the touch. If in doubt, insert a clean knife or wooden skewer into the centre of each sponge; it should come out clean.

To make the sugar syrup

While the sponges are baking, prepare the sugar syrup for soaking. Place the water, caster sugar and vanilla pod in a saucepan and bring to the boil. Simmer until all the sugar crystals have dissolved. Set aside to cool and then add the brandy.

Once the sponges are baked, let them rest for about 10 minutes outside of the oven. Using a pastry brush, soak the tops of the sponges with syrup while they are still warm; this allows the syrup to be absorbed faster.

Once just warm, run a knife all the way round the sides of the tins, remove the sponges from the tins and leave to cool completely on a wire cooling rack.

Once cool, wrap the sponges in cling film and then rest them overnight at room temperature. This will ensure that all the moisture is sealed in and the sponges firm up to the perfect texture for trimming and layering. When trimmed too soon after baking, the sponges tend to crumble and may even break into pieces.

To make the buttercream filling

Place the butter, icing sugar and salt into a mixing bowl and cream together until very pale and fluffy.

Add the dulce de leche to the mixture and stir through until combined and smooth.

To assemble the cake

Trim and sandwich together the three sponge layers using one-third of the buttercream filling and the brandy syrup for soaking. With the remaining buttercream filling, cover or mask the top and sides of the cake. For full instructions on how to do this, see pages 180–81.

To decorate

Cover the chilled cake with another generous layer of buttercream and, using a side-scraper with ridges, create a sculpted barrel design. If you are unable to achieve a perfect sculpted side on your first attempt, simply scrape off any excess buttercream and repeat the process until you are happy with the result, Clean up the top with a palette knife.

Chill until set. Dust the top of the cake liberally with cocoa powder before serving.

Serve the cake at room temperature. This cake is best enjoyed within 3 days of baking, but it can last for up to 1 week.

DARK CHOCOLATE TRUFFLE CAKE

THIS IS A RICH AND SMOOTH CHOCOLATE RECIPE THAT TASTES AT ITS BEST
WHEN SERVED AT ROOM TEMPERATURE. THE GANACHE GLAZE HAS A MELT-IN-THE-MOUTH
TEXTURE AND A SMELL THAT IS UTTERLY ADDICTIVE.
Makes one 15cm (6in) square cake, serving approximately 18 slices

ingredients

For the cake mix
250g plain chocolate (minimum 53% cocoa
solids), chopped or in buttons
335ml milk
570g soft light brown sugar
210g unsalted butter, softened
4 large eggs
365g plain flour
1 tsp baking powder
1 tsp bicarbonate of soda
Pinch of salt
15g cocoa powder
For the ganache
275ml whipping cream
350g plain chocolate (minimum 53% cocoa
solids), chopped or in buttons
30g glucose

equipment

Three 15cm (6in) square sandwich tins
Cake leveller or large serrated knife
Non-slip turntable
Flat disc to place on top of the turntable
(I use the loose base of a 30cm (12in)
springform cake tin)
15cm (6in) square cake card
Metal side scraper
Plastic piping bag
Metal star piping nozzle

Bake the sponge one day ahead of serving. Assemble and decorate the cake on the day of serving. Prepare the ganache filling a few hours before use, so it has time to set.

Preheat the oven to 160°C/gas mark 3.

Prepare the sandwich tins by greasing and lining them with greaseproof paper. For full instructions on how to do this, see page 87.

To make the cake
Place the chocolate, milk and 285g of the light brown sugar in a deep saucepan and bring to the boil, stirring with a spatula.

Place the butter and the remaining light brown sugar in a mixing bowl and cream together until pale and fluffy.

Beat the eggs lightly in another bowl and slowly add to the butter mixture while whisking quickly.

Sift the flour, baking powder, bicarbonate of soda, salt and cocoa powder together and add to the butter mixture in two batches. Mix together slowly until the batter is just combined.

Slowly pour the hot chocolate mix into the batter in a thin and steady stream, mixing at a medium speed. Scrape the bottom of the mixing bowl with a rubber spatula to make sure the batter is well combined.

Immediately pour the sponge mix into the lined cake tins and bake for 30–40 minutes, depending on your oven. The sponge is cooked when the sides are beginning to shrink away

TO DECORATE THE TOP EDGE, PIPE A SERIES OF S-SCROLLS AND C-SCROLLS. FOR THE BOTTOM EDGE, PIPE A BORDER OF SHELLS.

from the edges of the tin and the top springs back to the touch. Once cooked, the texture of this chocolate cake is slightly sticky and dense. If you insert a clean knife or wooden skewer into the centre of the sponge, it should come out with a small amount of crumb sticking to it.

Once the sponge is baked, let it rest for about 30 minutes outside of the oven.

Once just warm, run a knife all the way round the sides of the tin, remove the cake from the tin and leave to cool completely on a wire cooling rack.

Once cool, wrap the sponge in cling film and then rest it overnight at room temperature. This will ensure that all the moisture is sealed in and the sponge firms up to the perfect texture for trimming and layering. When trimmed too soon after baking, the sponge tends to crumble and may even break into pieces.

To make the ganache
Place the cream in a saucepan and bring to a bare simmer.

Place the chocolate and glucose into a bowl and pour the hot cream over the top. Whisk together until smooth. Once combined, leave to set at room temperature; the ganache should have the consistency of soft butter.

To assemble the cake
Using the cake leveller or serrated knife, trim the top and bottom crusts off the sponge. Slice the trimmed sponge into three horizontal layers of equal depth.

Sandwich together the three sponge layers using the ganache. With one-third of the ganache, cover or crumb-coat the top and sides of the cake. For full instructions on how to do this, see pages 180–81. Working with a square cake is slightly trickier than a round as you must cover each of the four sides separately. Chill until set.

To glaze the cake
Place the cake on a wire cooling rack and slide a tray underneath. Warm the remaining ganache to a thick pouring consistency. Pour the warmed ganache over the top of the cake ensuring the sides are evenly covered. Tap the tray to spread out the ganache and pop any air bubbles that appear. Chill the cake until set.

To decorate
Place the cake either on a cakestand or on top of the turntable covered with a piece of greaseproof paper.

Take the ganache caught in the tray and whisk it by hand until it stiffens slightly. Place a star nozzle into a plastic piping bag and fill with a small amount of the stiffened ganache. Pipe a border of S-scrolls and C-scrolls all around the edges of the cake top, Pipe a border of shells all around the bottom edge. For full instructions on how to do this, see page 185. If the cake has been placed on greaseproof paper, chill until the piped borders are set before transferring to a cakestand.

Serve the cake at room temperature. This cake is best enjoyed within 3 days of baking, but it can last for up to 1 week.

WHITE CHOCOLATE PASSION CAKE

THIS CAKE HAS AN EXOTIC FLAVOUR COMBINATION. AT FIRST BITE,
YOU TASTE THE SWEETEST WHITE CHOCOLATE BUT THEN THE PUNCHY PASSION FRUIT
JAM BURSTS IN YOUR MOUTH. DECORATE WITH PIPED SWAGS AND
PRETTY CANDLES FOR A SIMPLE YET SOPHISTICATED BIRTHDAY CAKE.

Makes one 15cm (6in) round cake, serving approximately 12 slices

ingredients

For the cake mix
125g white chocolate, chopped or in buttons
170ml milk
60g soft light brown sugar
225g caster sugar
105g unsalted butter, softened
2 large eggs
215g plain flour
1 tsp baking powder
Pinch of salt

For the chocolate buttercream
50ml whipping cream
65g white chocolate, chopped or in buttons
55g unsalted butter, softened
55g icing sugar, sifted

For the filling
2 tbsp Peggy's Passion fruit Jam or any other
good-quality passion fruit jam

equipment

Basic baking kit (see page 172)
Three 15cm (6in) round sandwich tins
Cake leveller or large serrated knife
Non-slip turntable
Flat disc to place on top of the turntable
(I use the loose base of a 30cm (12in)
springform cake tin)
15cm (6in) round cake card
Metal side scraper
Plastic piping bag
Plain round 4mm piping nozzle

Bake the sponges one day ahead of serving. Prepare the buttercream filling and assemble and decorate the cake on the day of serving.

Preheat the oven to 160°C/gas mark 3.

Prepare the sandwich tins by greasing and lining them with greaseproof paper. For full instructions on how to do this, see page 87.

To make the cake
Place the white chocolate, milk, light brown sugar and 85g of the caster sugar in a deep saucepan and bring to the boil, stirring with a spatula.

Place the butter and the remaining caster sugar in a mixing bowl and cream together until pale and fluffy.

Beat the eggs lightly in another bowl and slowly add to the butter mixture while whisking quickly.

Sift the flour, baking powder and salt together and add to the butter mixture in two batches. Mix together at a slow speed until the batter is just combined.

Slowly pour the hot chocolate mix into the batter in a thin and steady stream, mixing at a medium speed. Scrape the bottom of the mixing bowl with a rubber spatula to make sure the batter is well combined.

Immediately pour the sponge mix into the lined cake tins, dividing the batter evenly. If you find it difficult to measure by eye, use your kitchen scales to weigh out the amount of cake mixture for each tin.

DIVIDE THE TOP EDGE INTO TWELVE EQUAL SEGMENTS, THEN PIPE A BORDER
OF DOUBLE SWAGS FINISHED OFF WITH DOTS.

Bake for 25–30 minutes, depending on your oven. If you are using deeper cake tins, the sponges will take longer to cook. The sponges are cooked when the sides are beginning to shrink away from the edges of the tins and the tops are golden brown and spring back to the touch. If in doubt, insert a clean knife or wooden skewer into the centre of each sponge; it should come out clean.

Once the sponges are baked, let them rest for about 30 minutes outside of the oven. Once just warm, run a knife all the way round the sides of the tin, remove the cake from the tin and leave to cool completely on a wire cooling rack.

Once cool, wrap the sponges in cling film and then rest it overnight at room temperature. This will ensure that all the moisture is sealed in and the sponges firm up to the perfect texture for trimming and layering. When trimmed too soon after baking, the sponges tend to crumble and may even break into pieces.

To make the chocolate buttercream
Place the cream in a saucepan and bring to a bare simmer.

Place the white chocolate in a bowl and pour the hot cream over the top. Whisk together until smooth. Once combined, leave to set at room temperature; the white chocolate ganache should have the consistency of very soft butter.

Place the butter and icing sugar in a mixing bowl and cream together until pale and fluffy. One spoonful at a time, add the white chocolate ganache to the mixture and stir through until well combined.

To assemble the cake
Trim and sandwich together the three sponge layers using the passion fruit jam. Reserve 1 tablespoon of the chocolate buttercream for the piped decoration, then with the remaining buttercream, cover or mask the top and sides of the cake. For full instructions on how to do this, see pages 180–81. Chill until set.

To decorate
Place the cake either on a cakestand or on top of the turntable covered with a piece of greaseproof paper.

Place a round nozzle into a plastic piping bag and fill with the remaining buttercream. Divide the top of the cake into 12 equal segments. At the top edge, pipe a series of double swags all round the sides, revolving the turntable as necessary. To finish, pipe dots on top of the swag joints and pipe a row of dots all around the bottom edge of the cake. For full instructions on how to do this, see page 185. If the cake has been placed on greaseproof paper, chill until the piped dots are set before transferring to a cakestand.

Serve the cake at room temperature. This cake is best enjoyed within 3 days of baking, but it can last for up to 1 week.

SCRUMPTIOUS CARROT CAKE

AN EXCEPTIONALLY MOIST, PERFECTLY BALANCED CAKE BAKED WITH CHUNKS OF JUICY
PINEAPPLE AS WELL AS CARROTS AND WALNUTS. WONDERFUL WITH LEMON BUTTERCREAM,
IT CAN ALSO BE BAKED IN A LOAF TIN AND ENJOYED ON ITS OWN.

Makes one 15cm (6in) round cake, serving 8–12 slices

ingredients

For the cake mix
140ml vegetable oil
200g light brown sugar
80ml beaten eggs
(approximately 1½ small eggs)
80g walnuts, toasted and finely chopped
320g carrots, peeled and grated
280g tinned pineapple, drained and crushed
290g plain flour
¾ tsp bicarbonate of soda
¾ tsp baking powder
¾ tsp ground cinnamon
Pinch of salt
Seeds of 1 vanilla pod
For the buttercream filling
125g unsalted butter, softened
125g icing sugar, sifted
Finely grated zest of a unwaxed lemon
Pinch of salt
For the decoration
150g white sugar paste
1 tsp gum tragacanth
Small amount of white vegetable fat
Orange, green, blue and brown
paste food colour
Small amount of clear alcohol or edible glue

equipment

Basic baking kit (see page 172)
Three 15cm (6in) round sandwich tins
Cake leveller or large serrated knife
Non-slip turntable
Flat disc to place on top of the turntable
(I use the loose base of a 30cm (12in)
springform cake tin)
15cm (6in) round cake card
Metal side scraper
Plastic piping bag
Plain round 4mm (¼in) piping nozzle
To make the appliqué blossoms, see the
equipment list on page 176

Bake the sponges one day ahead of serving. Prepare the buttercream filling and assemble and decorate the cake on the day of serving.

Preheat the oven to 180°C/gas mark 4.

Prepare the sandwich tins by greasing and lining them with greaseproof paper. For full instructions on how to do this, see page 87.

To make the cake
Place the vegetable oil and light brown sugar in a mixing bowl and beat together. Beat the eggs lightly in another bowl and gradually add to the oil mixture until you get a smooth emulsion. Add the walnuts, carrots and pineapple and gently mix until well combined.

Sift the flour, bicarbonate of soda, baking powder, ground cinnamon and salt together and add to the wet mixture in two batches. Mix together at a slow speed until the batter is just combined.

Divide the batter evenly between the sandwich tins. If you find it difficult to measure by eye, use your kitchen scales to weigh out the amount of sponge mixture for each tin.

Bake for 40–50 minutes, depending on your oven. If you are using deeper cake tins, the sponges will take longer to cook. The sponges are cooked when the sides are beginning to shrink away from the edges of the tins and the tops are golden brown and spring back to the touch. If in doubt, insert a clean knife or wooden skewer into the centre of each sponge; it should come out clean.

MAKE APPLIQUÉ BLOSSOM DECORATIONS FROM SUGAR PASTE IN AN ASSORTMENT OF COLOURS, LAYERING DIFFERENT SIZES AND SHAPES TO MAKE EACH FLOWER.

Once the sponges are baked, let them rest for about 10 minutes outside of the oven. Once just warm, remove the sponges from the tins and leave to cool completely on a wire cooling rack.

Once cool, wrap the sponges in cling film and then rest overnight at room temperature. This will ensure that all the moisture is sealed in and the sponges firm up to the perfect texture for trimming and layering. When trimmed too soon after baking, the sponges tend to crumble and may even break into pieces.

To make the buttercream filling
Place the butter, icing sugar, lemon zest and salt in a mixing bowl and cream together until very pale and fluffy.

To assemble the cake
Trim and sandwich together the three sponge layers using one-third of the lemon buttercream filling. With the remaining buttercream filling, cover or mask the top and sides of the cake. For full instructions on how to do this, see pages 180–81. Chill until set.

To decorate
Following the instructions on page 176, make a selection of appliqué blossoms.

Place the cake either on to a cakestand or on top of the turntable covered with a piece of greaseproof paper.

Arrange the decorations around the sides of the cake and stick them down with a dab of buttercream. Trim away any overlap with a kitchen knife.

Place a round nozzle into a plastic piping bag and fill with the remaining buttercream. Around the sides, pipe rows of dots in between the blossoms, revolving the turntable as necessary. To finish, pipe a border of shells all around the top and bottom edges of the cake. For full instructions on how to do this, see page 185. If the cake has been placed on greaseproof paper, chill until the piped borders are set before transferring to a cakestand.

Serve the cake at room temperature.

GLORIOUS VICTORIA CAKE

BASED ON A CLASSIC VICTORIA SPONGE, THE KEY TO THIS SIMPLY DELICIOUS CAKE'S SUCCESS IS USING THE BEST QUALITY INGREDIENTS. FOR ADDED FLAVOUR AND MOISTURE, SOAK THE SPONGE LAYERS IN VANILLA SUGAR SYRUP. THE DESIGN IS INSPIRED BY THE ERA OF THE CAKE'S ORIGIN, DECORATED USING A VICTORIAN-STYLE SCROLL AND SHELL PIPING TECHNIQUE.

Makes one 15cm (6in) round cake, serving 8–12 slices

ingredients

For the sponge
200g unsalted butter, softened
200g caster sugar
Pinch of salt
Seeds of ½ vanilla pod
4 medium eggs
200g self-raising flour

For the sugar syrup
150ml water
150g caster sugar
Scraped vanilla pod

For the buttercream filling
300g unsalted butter, softened
300g icing sugar, sifted
Pinch of salt
Seeds of ½ vanilla pod
Small amount of pink food paste colour
3 tbsp any good-quality raspberry jam

equipment

Three 15cm (6in) round sandwich tins
Cake leveller or large serrated knife
Non-slip turntable
Flat disc to place on top of the turntable
(I use the loose base of a 30cm (12in) springform cake tin)
15cm (6in) round cake card
Metal side scraper
Two plastic piping bags
Medium star piping nozzle
Plain round 4mm (¼in) piping nozzle

Bake the sponges one day ahead of serving. Make the sugar syrup whilst baking the sponges. Prepare the buttercream filling and assemble and decorate the cake on the day of serving.

Preheat the oven to 175°C/gas mark 4.

Prepare the sandwich tins by greasing and lining them with greaseproof paper. For full instructions on how to do this, see page 87.

To make the sponge
Place the butter, sugar, salt and vanilla seeds in a mixing bowl and cream together until pale and fluffy.

Beat the eggs lightly in another bowl and slowly add to the butter mixture while whisking quickly. If the mixture starts to separate or curdle, stop adding the egg and beat in 2–3 tablespoons of the flour. This will rebind the batter. Once all the egg has been added and combined with the butter mixture, sift in the flour and stir until the batter is just combined. This will ensure the sponges stay light and fluffy.

Divide the batter evenly between the sandwich tins. If you find it difficult to measure by eye, use your kitchen scales to weigh out the amount of sponge mixture for each tin.

Bake for 15–20 minutes, depending on your oven. If you are using deeper cake tins, the sponges will take longer to cook. The sponges are cooked when the sides are beginning to shrink away from the edges of the tins and the tops are golden brown and spring back to the touch. If in doubt, insert a clean knife or wooden skewer into the centre of each sponge; it should come out clean.

IN RESPECT TO THE ORIGINS OF THIS CLASSIC SPONGE, DECORATE THE CAKE WITH A SELECTION OF VICTORIAN-STYLE PIPED SCROLLS.

To make the sugar syrup

While the sponges are baking, prepare the sugar syrup for soaking. Place the water, caster sugar and vanilla pod into a saucepan and bring to the boil. Simmer until all the sugar crystals have dissolved. Set aside to cool down slightly. Discard the vanilla pod.

Once the sponges are baked, let them rest for about 10 minutes outside of the oven. Using a pastry brush, soak the tops of the sponges with vanilla bean sugar syrup while they are still warm; this allows the syrup to be absorbed faster.

Once just warm, run a knife all the way round the sides of the tins, remove the sponges from the tins and leave to cool completely on a wire cooling rack.

Once cool, wrap the sponges in cling film and then rest them overnight at room temperature. This will ensure that all the moisture is sealed in and the sponges firm up to the perfect texture for trimming and layering. When trimmed too soon after baking, the sponges tend to crumble and may even break into pieces.

To make the buttercream filling

Place the butter, icing sugar, salt and vanilla seeds into a mixing bowl and cream together until very pale and fluffy.

Add a small amount of pink food colour to the mixture and stir through until combined and the buttercream is a pastel shade.

To assemble the cake

Trim and sandwich together the three sponge layers using one layer of buttercream filling and one layer of raspberry jam, and the vanilla sugar syrup for soaking. With the remaining buttercream filling, cover or mask the top and sides of the cake. For full instructions on how to do this, see pages 180–81.

To decorate

Place the cake either on to a cakestand or on top of the turntable covered with a piece of greaseproof paper.

Place a star nozzle into a plastic piping bag and fill with a generous amount of the remaining buttercream. Place a round nozzle into another plastic piping bag and fill with a small amount of the remaining buttercream.

Divide the top of the cake into eight equal segments. Using the star nozzle, pipe a ring of C-scrolls around the circumference, revolving the turntable as necessary. Next, pipe a shell from the middle of each C-scroll towards the centre. Where all eight shells meet, pipe a rosette on top at the centre of the cake top. Using the round nozzle, pipe a small dot between each shell.

Using the star nozzle, pipe eight fleur de lys evenly around the sides at the top edge, with a single upside-down shell underneath at the bottom edge. To finish, pipe a small dot between the fleur de lys and shell. For full instructions on how to do this, see page 185. If the cake has been placed on greaseproof paper, chill until the piped dots are set before transferring to a cakestand.

Serve the cake at room temperature. This cake is best enjoyed within 3 days of baking, but it can last for up to 1 week.

CLASSIC
CAKES & BAKES

NEAPOLITAN MARBLE CAKE

A DELICIOUS MARBLE CAKE BRINGS BACK FONDEST CHILDHOOD MEMORIES. IT NOT ONLY TASTES JUST LIKE THE ONE GRANDMA USED TO MAKE, BUT LOOKS VERY PRETTY INSIDE WHEN CUT. I HAVE REVIVED THIS RETRO CLASSIC BY ADDING A PALE PINK SPONGE SWIRL INTO THE MIX AND USING A TRADITIONAL BUNDT CAKE TIN IN A CONTEMPORARY SHAPE.

Makes one 30cm (12in) cake, serving 16–20 slices

ingredients

For the sponge
250g unsalted butter, softened,
plus extra for greasing the cake tin
250g caster sugar
Pinch of salt
Seeds of 1 vanilla pod
5 medium eggs
250g self-raising flour, sifted
25g cocoa powder
25ml milk
Pink liquid food colour
Plain flour for dusting
Icing sugar for dusting
For the sugar syrup
150ml water
150g caster sugar

equipment

30cm (12in) Kugelhupf or Bundt cake tin

Preheat the oven to 175°C/gas mark 4. Prepare the cake tin by greasing with softened butter and dusting with plain flour.

To make the sponge
Place the butter, caster sugar, salt and vanilla seeds in a mixing bowl and cream together until pale and fluffy.

Beat the eggs lightly in another bowl and slowly add to the butter mixture while whisking quickly. If the mixture starts to separate or curdle, stop adding the egg and beat in 2–3 tablespoons of the flour. This will rebind the batter.

Once all the egg has been added and combined with the butter mixture, sift in the flour and stir until the batter is just combined.

Divide the batter into three equal parts. Mix the first with a small amount of pink food colour to create a pale pastel shade. Mix the second with the cocoa powder and add the milk. Keep the third plain.

Pour the pink batter into the bottom of the prepared cake tin, followed by the chocolate batter and then finally the plain batter.

To 'marble' the mixture, gently fold through all three coloured layers with a fork or spatula.

Bake for approximately 1 hour, depending on your oven. If you are using a deeper cake tin, the sponge will take longer to cook. To check if the sponge is cooked, insert a clean knife or wooden skewer into the centre of each sponge; it should come out clean.

To make the sugar syrup
While the sponge is baking, prepare the sugar syrup for soaking. Place the water and caster sugar into a saucepan and bring to the boil. Simmer until all the sugar crystals have dissolved. Set aside to cool down slightly.

Once the sponge is baked, let it rest for approximately 10 minutes outside of the oven. Using a pastry brush, soak the tops of the sponges with sugar syrup while it is still warm; this allows the syrup to be absorbed faster.

Once just warm, remove the sponge from the tin and leave to cool completely on a wire cooling rack.

Dust the top of the cake with icing sugar before serving at room temperature.

CHOCOLATE HAZELNUT TORTE

DURING A TRIP TO THE AUSTRIAN CITY OF SALZBURG, I CAME ACROSS A CAKE THAT WAS SO MOIST, NUTTY AND CHOCOLATEY, WITH A HINT OF RUM, THAT I COULDN'T GET ENOUGH OF IT. FOR ME IT WAS A SLICE OF CAKE HEAVEN, AN UNFORGETABLE EXPERIENCE THAT INSPIRED THIS RECIPE. I HOPE THAT YOU WON'T GET ENOUGH OF IT EITHER.

Makes one 20cm (8in) round cake, serving 8–12 slices

ingredients

For the torte
150g ground hazelnuts
75g plain chocolate (minimum 53% cocoa solids), chopped or in buttons
50g self-raising flour
1 tsp ground cinnamon
150g unsalted butter, softened
105g soft light brown sugar
Seeds of ½ vanilla pod
3 large eggs, separated
1½ tbsp dark rum
Pinch of salt
Pinch of cream of tartar
20g caster sugar
For the decoration
250g marzipan
250g ganache (see page 105)
Icing sugar for dusting
Cocoa powder for dusting

equipment

20cm (8in) round springform cake tin
Flat metal tray or disc (I use the loose base of a large 30cm (12in) springform cake tin)
Large serrated knife
Large step palette knife
Laser-cut cake stencil with wheatsheaf or leaf pattern

Preheat the oven to 150°C/gas mark 3.

Prepare the springform cake tin by lining it with greaseproof paper. For full instructions on how to do this, see page 87.

To make the torte
Place the hazelnuts, chocolate and flour in a food processor and grind until the mixture resembles coarse biscuit crumbs, but is not oily. Transfer to a mixing bowl, add the ground cinnamon and set aside.

Place the butter, light brown sugar and vanilla seeds in a mixing bowl and cream together until pale and fluffy.

Beat the eggs yolks lightly in another bowl and slowly add to the butter mixture while whisking quickly until well incorporated.

Fold half the ground hazelnut and chocolate mixture into the batter. Add the rum, then fold in the other half.

In a clean dry bowl, whisk the egg whites with the salt and cream of tartar until they reach soft peaks. Add the caster sugar and continue whisking until the meringue mixture is glossy but not dry.

Fold a tablespoonful of the meringue mixture into the batter to loosen it, then gently fold the rest in to keep the batter light.

Pour the batter into the prepared cake tin and level the surface using a palette knife or the back of a spoon.

Bake on a low shelf for 50–55 minutes, depending on your oven. The cake is cooked

FOR THE FINISHING TOUCH TO THIS TORTE, ROLL OUT THE MARZIPAN TO A THIN SHEET THEN POUR AND SPREAD THE GLOSSY GANACHE OVER THE TOP.

when the top is lightly browned and springs back to the touch. If in doubt, insert a clean knife or wooden skewer into the centre of the cake; it should come out clean.

Once the cake is baked, let it rest for about 30 minutes outside of the oven. Once cool, remove the cake from the tin when you are ready to decorate.

To decorate
On a surface dusted with icing sugar, roll the marzipan out to a thickness of 3–4mm (1). It must be large enough that you can cut a 20cm (8in) round from it. Place the rolled marzipan on a flat metal tray or disc (2).

Gently warm the ganache to a thick pouring consistency. Place the warmed ganache in a jug or bowl and tap the sides to release any air bubbles, which will rise to the top.

Slowly pour the ganache over the marzipan (3). Using a large step palette knife, spread it out evenly across the marzipan (4). If there are any air bubbles or lines, tap the metal tray to even out the surface. Chill in the fridge or freezer until the ganache has set.

If the top of the cake is uneven, level with a serrated knife and turn upside down so the perfectly flat side is facing upwards. Brush the top of the cake with a thin layer of ganache.

Remove the marzipan and ganache sheet from the fridge. Carefully cut out a 20cm (8in) round using a slightly warmed cutter (5). Peel away any excess and use a step palette knife to gently lift and place the round on top of the cake (6).

While the ganache is still firm and set, centre the stencil on the top of the ganache layer. Dust the surface liberally with cocoa powder. Carefully lift the stencil off the cake to reveal the pattern.

Serve the cake at room temperature.

LEMON, ALMOND AND POPPY SEED CAKE

A LIGHT AND ZINGY CAKE SPECKLED WITH POPPY SEEDS, WHICH NOT ONLY LOOK PRETTY BUT ALSO ADD A BIT OF CRUNCH TO THE TEXTURE. A DELICIOUSLY MOIST SPONGE, THIS CAKE WILL LAST FOR A FEW DAYS WHEN KEPT AT ROOM TEMPERATURE.

Makes one 25cm (10in) cake, serving 12–16 slices

ingredients

For the sponge
200g unsalted butter, softened,
plus extra for greasing the cake tin
Plain flour for dusting
200g caster sugar
4 medium eggs
200g self-raising flour
100g ground almonds
30g ground poppy seeds (you can grind
them yourself using a pestle and mortar)
Finely grated zest of 2 lemons
For the lemon syrup
100ml lemon juice
100g caster sugar
For the glaze
500g fondant patissiere
Juice of 1 lemon
1 tsp glucose

equipment

25cm (10in) Kugelhupf or Bundt cake tin

Preheat the oven to 175°C/gas mark 4. Prepare the cake tin by greasing with softened butter and dusting with plain flour.

To make the sponge
Place the butter, sugar and lemon zest in a mixing bowl and cream until pale and fluffy.

Beat the eggs lightly in another bowl and slowly add to the butter mixture while whisking quickly. If the mixture starts to separate or curdle, stop adding the egg and beat in 2–3 tablespoons of the flour. This will rebind the batter. Once all the egg has been added and combined with the butter mixture, sift in the flour and add the ground almonds and poppy seeds. Stir until the batter is just combined.

Pour the batter into the prepared cake tin, using a rubber spatula to help fill the tin. Before baking, tap the filled cake tin on your worksurface a few times to make sure the batter has reached all the cavities at the bottom of the tin.

Bake for 30–40 minutes, depending on your oven. The sponge is cooked when the sides are beginning to shrink away from the edges of the tin and the top is golden brown and springs back to the touch. If in doubt, insert a clean knife or wooden skewer into the centre of the sponge; it should come out clean.

To make the lemon syrup
While the sponge is baking, prepare a lemon syrup for soaking. Place the lemon juice and caster sugar into a saucepan and bring to the boil. Simmer until all the sugar crystals have dissolved. Set aside to cool down slightly.

Once the sponge is baked, immediately brush the sponge with half the lemon syrup; this allows the syrup to be absorbed faster.

Allow to cool for about 30 minutes outside of the oven. Once just warm, turn the cake out of the tin and leave to cool completely on a wire cooling rack. Brush the other side of the sponge with the remaining syrup.

To make the glaze
Gently warm the fondant patissiere with the lemon juice to a thick pouring consistency. Do not to allow it to boil, as it will lose its shine. Stir in the glucose. Pour the fondant glaze over the top of the cake and allow to set.

Serve at room temperature.

RASPBERRY & ROSE DOME CAKE

MADE OF THIN LAYERS OF JACONDE SPONGE FILLED WITH PURPLE RASPBERRY
AND ROSE JAM, VANILLA BUTTERCREAM AND FRESH RASPBERRIES,
THIS IS MY PERSONAL TAKE ON THE CLASSIC SWEDISH PRINCESS CAKE.
IT IS UTTERLY DELICIOUS AND PERFECT FOR AN OCCASION.
IT IS A DELICATE CAKE, SO KEEP THE DECORATION SIMPLE.
Makes one 15cm (6in) round dome cake, serving 8–12 slices
To make two dome cakes, simply double the amounts given below

ingredients

For the crème patissière
75g egg yolks
(approximately 3 small egg yolks)
125g caster sugar
1 vanilla pod
500ml whole milk
50g cornflour

For the Jaconde sponge
3 medium eggs
125g icing sugar
125g ground almonds
3 egg whites
15g sugar
40g plain flour

For the filling
250g unsalted butter, at room temperature
1 tbsp Eau de Vie (optional)
2 tbsp Peggy's Purple Raspberry and Rose
Jam or any other good-quality raspberry jam
Punnet of raspberries (approximately 150g)

For the decoration
400g marzipan
600g white sugar paste
Brown, green and pink paste food colour
1 tsp gum tragacanth
Small amount of white vegetable fat
1 tbsp apricot jam, sieved
Icing sugar for dusting
Small amount or clear alcohol,
such as vodka or Eau de Vie
Small amount of royal icing (see page 183)

equipment

Two baking trays with
a minimum width of 30cm (12in)
15cm (6in) sphere mould
(I use one half of a ball-shaped cake tin)
15cm (6in) round pastry cutter
Plastic piping bag
15cm (6in) round thin cake card
Paper piping bag (see page 184)
Small non-stick rolling pin
Dog rose silicon mould
(I use a mould from FPC Sugarcraft)
Primrose cutter (medium or large)
Blossom mould
(I use a mould from Blossom Sugar Art)
Egg carton or plastic paint palette with wells
Piece of ribbon, long enough to
cover the circumference of the cake
Plain round 2.5cm (1in) pastry cutter

1

2

3

4

5

6

7

8

9

10

11

12

13

14

15

16

This cake has a shelf life of 3 days when stored in the fridge, however the decoration may become soft and sticky in cold humid conditions. Therefore, I recommend making the cake no more than 2 days in advance of serving and consuming it within 1 day.

Preheat the oven to 220°C/gas mark 7.

Line two baking trays with baking parchment.

To make the crème patissière
Whisk the egg yolks with the caster sugar in a mixing bowl, then add the cornflour and stir to combine. Place the milk, vanilla seeds and scraped vanilla pod in a saucepan and bring to a bare simmer. Pour about a quarter of the hot milk onto the egg yolk mixture, immediately stirring until smooth.

Return the egg yolk and milk mixture to the pan with the remaining hot milk. Continue cooking until the mixture thickens and bubbles in the centre, stirring well to make sure the crème patissière does not burn on the base of the pan. Taste the crème patissière to check it is cooked; it should not taste floury. The texture should be smooth and thick.

Transfer to a bowl or tray. To prevent a skin from forming, cover tightly with cling film, pressing down firmly to make sure there are no air pockets. Allow to cool and chill until further use.

To make the Jaconde sponge
Beat the whole eggs and icing sugar together until pale and fluffy. Sift together the flour and ground almonds, then gently fold into the egg mixture using a spatula.

In a clean dry bowl, whisk the egg whites with the sugar until they reach soft peaks. Fold the meringue mixture into the batter.

Divide the batter evenly between the two prepared baking trays and level the surface using a palette knife or the back of a spoon.

Bake for 8–10 minutes on a low shelf, depending on your oven. The sponge is cooked when the sides are beginning to shrink away from the edges of the tin and the top is lightly browned and springs back to the touch.

Allow to cool outside of the oven but leave the sponges in the baking trays. Once cool, cover with cling film to prevent the sponge sheets from drying out.

To make the buttercream filling
Place the crème patissière in a bowl and beat, adding the softened butter little by little until all the butter is incorporated and the buttercream has thickened. Add the Eau de Vie.

To assemble the cake
Place the sphere mould on top of a small bowl to hold it steady. Line the inside of the mould with clingfilm, overlapping the edges (1).

Cut out a 30cm (12in) round from one of the sponge sheets (2–3). Use it to line the inside of the sphere mould, leaving a small overlap around the outside edge. Trim off any excess using a pair of kitchen scissors (4–7).

Fill a piping bag with the buttercream filling. Snip an inch off the tip and pipe a thick layer into the bottom of the cake mould, then place six fresh raspberries evenly over the buttercream (8). Pipe another layer of buttercream on top (9). Continue adding layers of buttercream and fresh raspberries until you have almost reached the top edge of the mould. Level off the last layer of buttercream using a palette knife (10).

Cut out two 15cm (6in) rounds from the remaining sponge sheet using a pastry cutter (11). Sandwich the two rounds of sponge together with a thin layer of raspberry jam (12–13). Place the two sponge rounds on top of the buttercream-filled mould (14). Spread over a thin layer of buttercream, then place the cake card on top. Trim any excess sponge from around the edges of the mould (15). Fold the overlapping cling film over the top (16). Chill for at least 4–6 hours or preferably overnight.

To make the decoration
While your cake is setting in the fridge, make the flower decorations. You can make sugar flowers well in advance and store them for several months in a cool and dry place, but do not store them in an airtight container as the paste may sweat and collapse.

For the mocha-coloured cake, mix 400g sugar paste with brown food colour to a very pale coffee shade. For the green cake, mix 400g sugar paste with green food colour to a pale pastel shade. To prevent it from drying out, keep the sugar paste wrapped in cling film until use.

Mix the remaining sugar paste with a little pink food colour and the gum tragacanth. Add a small amount of white vegetable fat to make the paste smooth and pliable. For the mocha cake, mix only one shade of pale pink. For the green cake, mix a few different shades of pink. Wrap the sugar paste in cling film and allow to rest for 30 minutes in order to firm up a little.

To make the blossoms for the mocha-coloured cake, follow the instructions on page 174 using the primrose blossom cutter and mould.

To make the dog roses for the green cake, rub a thin layer of vegetable fat into the mould and press a small ball of pink sugar paste into the embossed floral shape. Smooth and flatten the back with your fingers and, if necessary, trim off any excess paste using a small kitchen knife. To release, bend the mould outwards until the flower drops out. For a similar technique, see page 174. Place the sugar flower on a curved surface, for example, inside the wells of a paint palette or an egg carton lined with greaseproof paper, to dry. Make 3–4 flowers in different shades of pink sugar paste using this method.

To decorate

Once the cake has set, remove it from the fridge and turn it out on a sheet of greaseproof paper. Remove the mould and the cling film **(1)**.

Gently warm the apricot jam and brush a thin layer all over the dome cake **(2)**.

On a surface dusted with icing sugar, roll the marzipan out to a thickness 3–4mm. It must be large enough to cover the dome. Using a rolling pin, lift the rolled marzipan and lay it over the dome cake **(3)**. Smooth the marzipan down the sides of the dome using your fingers. Tuck the edges down and trim away any excess

marzipan using a kitchen knife **(4)**.

Splash some clear alcohol onto your hands **(5)**. Smooth the alcohol over the marzipan-covered dome **(6)**. This creates an adhesive. Roll out the coloured sugar paste and place over the marzipan the same way **(7)**. Trim away any excess sugar paste as before **(8)**.

For the mocha dome cake, use a piece of ribbon to determine the correct circumference of the base of the dome **(9)**. Using this ribbon as a guide for length and a ruler for depth, roll out a thin strip of the remaining pink sugar paste **(10)**. Cut a 2.5cm (1in) wide strip that is long enough to go all around the base of the dome **(11)**. Using a small round cutter, cut out even half-circles from the pink sugar paste strip to create a swag border **(12)**.

Brush the base of the dome thinly with clear alcohol **(13)**. Lay the pink sugar paste strip all around it, with the cut-out edge pointing upwards **(14)**.

Mix the royal icing with brown food colour to make a dark chocolate shade with a soft-peak consistency (see pages 182–3). Fill a paper piping bag with the icing, snip a small hole from the tip of the bag and pipe a swag border following the edge of the pink icing **(15)**. Pipe three loops at the highest points of the swags with a dot below **(16)**. Although not essential, this is best done using a turntable.

To finish, pipe small brown dots into the centre of each pink blossom. Using a tiny amount of royal icing, stick a cluster of three blossoms on the top of the dome.

For the green dome cake, mix the royal icing with pink food colour to make a pale shade with a soft-peak consistency (see page 182–183). Fill a paper piping bag with the icing, snip a small hole from the tip of the bag and pipe double swags evenly around the base of the dome and finish with a dot at all the joints.

To finish, using a tiny amount of royal icing, stick a few randomly placed dog roses on top of the dome.

MINI EGGNOG KUGELHOPFS

BASED ON A TRADITIONAL BAVARIAN RECIPE, THESE LITTLE CAKES
ARE PERFECT WITH AN AFTERNOON CUP OF COFFEE.
THE WORD 'KUGEL' MEANS DOME IN GERMAN, REFLECTING THE
CLASSIC SHAPE TIN THESE CAKES ARE BAKED IN.

Makes 12 individual kugelhopfs

ingredients

Small amount of unsalted butter, softened for
greasing the cake moulds
6 medium eggs
265g icing sugar, sifted
Seeds of 1 vanilla pod
300ml vegetable oil
300ml Advocaat
150g plain flour, sifted plus extra for dusting
150g cornflour, sifted
12g baking powder
Pinch of salt
160ml Advocaat, plus extra for serving
(optional)
160ml rum
Icing sugar for dusting

equipment

Two mini Kugelhopf trays, each with 6 moulds
approximately 10cm (4in) in diameter

Preheat the oven to 200°C/gas mark 5.
Prepare the cake moulds by greasing with
softened butter and dusting with plain flour.

Place the eggs, icing sugar and vanilla
seeds in the bowl of an electric mixer and
whisk together until pale and fluffy. Add the
vegetable oil and the eggnog and mix until
just combined.

Sift the flour, cornflour and baking powder
together and gently fold it through the egg
mixture.

Divide the batter evenly between the
Kugelhopf trays, filling each mould until two-
thirds full only. If you find it difficult to measure
by eye, use your kitchen scales to weigh out
the amount of cake mixture for each mould.

Place the tray in the oven and turn the

temperature down to 180°C/gas mark 4. Bake
for 15 minutes, then turn the tray around and
bake for a further 10–15 minutes. The cakes
are cooked when the sides are beginning to
shrink away from the edges of the moulds and
the tops are golden brown and spring back
to the touch. If in doubt, insert a clean knife
or wooden skewer into the centre of each
cake; it should come out clean. Once the cakes
are baked, let them rest for a few minutes
outside of the oven before turning them out
of the moulds.

Combine the rum and Advocaat, then using a
pastry brush, soak the tops of the cakes with
the alcohol while they are still warm. Leave to
cool completely on a wire cooling rack.

Serve at room temperature. Dust the tops of
the cakes with icing sugar before serving. If
preferred, serve with a drop of extra Advocaat.

CHOCOLATE BATTENBERG CAKE

A CONTEMPORARY TWIST ON A TRADITIONAL DESIGN, THE DARK AND LIGHT SQUARES REMIND ME OF SMALL CHEQUERBOARDS AND THIS CAKE WOULD BE GREAT FOR A QUEEN OF HEARTS TEA PARTY. IT TASTES DELICIOUS, TOO!

Makes 3 rectangular cakes of approximately 20cm (8in) long, serving 8 slices each

ingredients

250g unsalted butter, softened
250g caster sugar
Seeds of 1 vanilla pod
235g self-raising flour
100g ground almonds
45g cocoa powder
6 medium eggs
1 heaped tbsp apricot jam, sieved
750g marzipan
Brown paste food colour
Icing sugar, for dusting

equipment

Two 20cm (8in) square cake tins
Pair of cake smoothers
Marzipan crimper

Bake the sponges one day ahead of assembling and serving.

Preheat the oven to 180°C/gas mark 4. Prepare the cake tins by lining them with greaseproof paper. For full instructions on how to do this, see page 87.

To make the sponge
Place the butter, caster sugar and vanilla seeds in a mixing bowl and cream together until pale and fluffy.

Beat the eggs lightly in a jug and slowly pour into the butter mixture while mixing on high speed to incorporate.

Divide the batter into two equal parts. Sift 140g flour and 50g almonds together and fold through the first half of the batter. Then sift 95g flour, 50g almonds and the cocoa powder together and fold through the second half. Pour each batter into a prepared cake tin.

Bake for 25–30 minutes, depending on your oven. The sponges are cooked when the sides are beginning to shrink away from the edges of the tin and the tops spring back to the touch. If in doubt, insert a clean knife or wooden skewer into the centre of the sponge; it should come out clean.

Allow to cool for about 30 minutes outside of the oven. Once just warm, turn the cakes out of the tins and leave to cool completely on a wire cooling rack. Once cool, wrap the sponges in cling film and then rest them overnight at room temperature. This will ensure that the sponges firm up to the perfect texture for trimming and layering. When trimmed too soon after baking, the sponges tend to crumble and may even break into pieces.

To assemble the cake
Level the tops of the sponges using a serrated knife to an overall height of 2.5cm (1in). Trim off the edges and cut each sponge into three even strips of about 5cm (2in) wide so you have three white and three brown sponge pieces all of the same size. For each Battenberg cake you need one brown and one white piece of sponge.

Gently warm the apricot jam and spread a thin layer over one of the dark sponges (1). Place one of the light sponges on top, then cut them in half lengthwise and lay flat (2). Brush another thin layer of jam over the surface of one half slice and then place the second half slice on top, with the colours facing the opposite way to create a grid of four squares when viewed from the front. Repeat for the other pieces of sponge or, alternatively, freeze them for later use.

THE CHEQUERBOARD EFFECT OF THE CAKE IS CREATED BY LAYERING TWO COLOURS OF SPONGE. THE SIMPLE MARZIPAN COVERING IS GIVEN ADDED VISUAL INTEREST USING CRIMPERS.

Mix the marzipan with the brown food colour to a light shade. On a surface dusted with icing sugar, roll the marzipan out to a thickness of 3–4mm. It must be large enough that you can cut a 20cm (8in) square. Using a ruler and kitchen knife, cut out a 20cm (8in) square (3). Flip it over onto a clean surface or sheet of greaseproof paper (4). Spread a thin layer of jam over the marzipan sheet (5). Place the sponge log on top of the marzipan towards one side. If necessary, trim the marzipan sheet to the same length as the log (6). Making sure the ends meet at one of the corners, carefully wrap the marzipan around the log (7). Trim away any excess. Gently press the join together with your fingers.

Square up the sides by gently pressing them with the cake smoothers (8). For extra detail, crimp along the top corners using a marzipan crimper (9).

TRIPLE BERRY CHEESECAKES

THESE STUNNING LITTLE CHEESECAKES ARE VERY EASY TO MAKE AND TASTE FABULOUS. THEY HAVE A VERY LIGHT TEXTURE AND CONSIST OF LAYERS OF STRAWBERRY, RASPBERRY AND BLUEBERRY.

Makes 16 individual cheesecakes

ingredients

For the biscuit base
100g melted butter
2 tbsp runny honey
200g digestive biscuits, finely crushed
1 tsp ground cinnamon
For the cheesecake
6 gelatine leaves (I use Supercook Platinum)
100ml blueberry purée
100ml raspberry purée
100ml strawberry purée
(if you can't find berry purées, make your own by puréeing fresh berries in a blender and passing them through a fine sieve)
620g full-fat cream cheese
185g caster sugar
210g crème fraîche
640ml double or whipping cream

equipment

Sixteen 5cm (2in) round dessert rings or mousse moulds
5cm (2in) deep acetate strips
Three plastic piping bags

Line the insides of the dessert rings or mousse moulds with the acetate strips.

To make the biscuit base
Melt the butter with the honey in a saucepan. Add the crushed biscuits and cinnamon and mix until combined. Carefully press a tablespoonful of the biscuit mixture into the bottom of each mould, keeping the sides as clean as possible.

To make the cheesecake
Place the gelatine leaves into a bowl and soak them in cold water. Gently warm each of the fruit purées separately, squeeze the water from the gelatine leaves and dissolve two leaves in each of the hot fruit purées. Set aside to cool.

Place the cream cheese and caster sugar in a bowl and mix together until smooth and combined. Then add the crème fraîche. Whip the cream to a soft-peak consistency, taking care not to overwhip.

Divide the cream cheese mixture into three equal parts. Once the fruit purées have cooled to room temperature, mix each one separately with a third of the cream cheese mixture, using a whisk. From this point, you must work quickly as the gelatine can set.

Divide the whipped cream into three equal parts. Gently fold through each of the three cream cheese mixtures until combined.

Starting with strawberry, followed by raspberry and then blueberry, layer the three fruit mixtures in the lined rings or moulds. I find it easier and neater to use piping bags to create the different layers. However, if you do not have piping bags you can carefully spoon the mixtures into the moulds instead.

If using piping bags, fill a plastic piping bag with each mixture. Snip 2.5cm (1in) from the tip of the bag and pipe a layer over the bottom of the biscuit base to about halfway up the sides. Repeat for the two other fruit mixtures until you reach the top.

Flatten the top layers with a palette knife or the back of a spoon. Chill for at least 4 hours or until set.

You can make these cheesecakes up to 3 days in advance if stored in the fridge. De-mould and remove the acetate strips just before serving.

BANANA LOAF CAKE WITH BANANA FROSTING

FOR MAXIMUM FLAVOUR USE OVER-RIPE BANANAS AND ENJOY THE CAKE ONE DAY AFTER BAKING SO THE FLAVOURS HAVE TIME TO MATURE.

Makes 1 large loaf cake, serving 8–12 slices

ingredients

100g butter, softened plus extra for greasing
200g light brown sugar
1 tsp ground cinnamon
2 medium eggs
300g over-ripe bananas
180g plain flour
1 tsp bicarbonate of soda
60g plain chocolate (minimum 53% cocoa solids), chopped or in buttons
80g walnuts, toasted and roughly chopped
For the banana frosting
See page 56

equipment

Large 23cm x 13cm (9in x 5in) loaf tin

Preheat the oven to 175°C/gas mark 4.

Prepare the loaf tin by greasing it with butter.

To make the cake
Place the butter, light brown sugar and ground cinnamon in a mixing bowl and cream together until pale and fluffy.

Beat the eggs lightly and slowly add to the butter mixture while mixing on high speed to incorporate.

Mash up the bananas and add to the batter, followed by the chocolate and walnuts.

Sift the flour and bicarbonate of soda together and add to the batter on low speed until just combined. Pour the batter into the prepared cake tin.

Bake for 35–40 minutes, depending on your oven. The cake is cooked when the top springs back to the touch. If in doubt, insert a clean knife or wooden skewer into the centre of the cake; it should come out clean.

Allow to cool for a few minutes outside of the oven before turning the cake out of the tin. Leave to cool completely on a wire cooling rack.

To make the frosting
Following the instructions on page 58, make the banana frosting.

Once cool, spread the top of the cake with the frosting using a palette knife. Chill for about 30 minutes to set the frosting.

Serve at room temperature.

LIGHT LUXURY FRUIT CAKE

LIGHT AND MOIST WITH FRUITY FLAVOURS, THIS CAKE HAS AN ADDITIONAL
CRUNCH FROM THE DRIED FIGS. TO CREATE A CONTEMPORARY CHRISTMAS CAKE
WITH A SENSE OF OPULENCE, I TOOK INSPIRATION FROM THE WORLD OF
INTERIOR DESIGN AND USED DAMASK STENCILS, OVALS AND STAGS WITH GOLD LUSTRE.
USING STENCILS WITH ROYAL ICING LOOKS SCARIER THAN IT IS, I SUGGEST
TESTING IT ON A PIECE OF PAPER FIRST TO GET A FEELING FOR THE
TECHNIQUE BEFORE DECORATING THE CAKE.

Makes one 15cm x 20cm (6in x 8in) oval cake, serving 20 finger slices

ingredients

For the fruit mix
150g raisins
65g dried cranberries, halved
230g sultanas, roughly chopped
120g whole glacé cherries
80g dried figs, chopped
25g sour cherries, chopped
60ml whisky
50g golden syrup
Grated zest of 1 lemon

For the cake mix
120g eggs (approximately 2 small eggs)
90g dark brown sugar
115g unsalted butter, softened
25g ground almonds
90g plain flour
¼ tsp ground cinnamon
Pinch of ground cloves
Pinch of ground nutmeg
Pinch of salt
30ml whisky for soaking

For the decoration
1 tbsp apricot jam, sieved
600g marzipan
800g ivory sugar paste
250g white florists paste
Small amount of white vegetable fat
Ivory and brown food paste colour
Small amount of edible gold lustre
Small amount of cocoa powder
(for the brown stag only)
About 150g royal icing
Small amount of clear alcohol,
such as vodka or Eau de Vie
Small amount of piping gel
Icing sugar, for dusting

equipment

15cm x 20cm (6in x 8in) oval cake card
20cm x 25cm (8in x 10in) oval cake board
Approximately 1.5m of 15mm-wide satin
ribbon to cover the base of the cake and board
Small piece of double-sided sticky tape
15cm x 20cm (6in x 8in) oval cake tin
Newspaper and string for insulating cake tin
Pair of marzipan spacers
Pair of cake smoothers
Paper piping bag
Laser-cut damask cake stencil
Oval cutter of about 12cm x 8cm (5in x 3in)
Silicon stag mould (I use a mould
from First Impressions)
Large soft powder brush
Fine artist's brush

Make this cake at least 3–4 days in advance and store it wrapped in a layer of greaseproof paper, then in aluminium foil, to preserve moisture and flavour. You can make it several weeks, if not months, in advance if stored in a cool dry place. For an extra-moist and boozy flavour, feed the cake with whisky on a weekly basis or several times before icing.

To make the fruit mix
Place all the ingredients for the fruit mix into a large bowl, stir well and cover with cling film. Leave to infuse overnight at room temperature.

Preheat the oven to 140°C/gas mark 1. Double-line a deep 15cm (6in) round or oval cake tin with greaseproof paper and wrap the tin with a double thickness of brown paper, securing it with string.

To make the cake mix
Place the eggs and sugar in a medium bowl and whisk by hand until combined.

In a separate bowl, cream together the butter and the ground almonds until just creamy but not too aerated. Slowly add the egg mixture until you have a smooth emulsion. If the mixture starts to separate or curdle, add 1 tablespoon of flour. This will rebind the batter.

Sift the remaining dry ingredients together and fold through the batter in two batches until just combined.

Add the infused fruit to the cake mix and combine thoroughly and evenly with either a spatula or clean, gloved hands.

Pour the cake mix into the prepared tin. Level the surface with the back of a spoon. Before baking, tap the filled cake tin on your worksurface a few times to release any large air bubbles. This prevents the surface of the cake cracking.

Bake on a low shelf for 2–3 hours, depending on your oven. To prevent the cake from over-browning, place an empty tray on the rack above. The cake is cooked when the top is golden brown. If in doubt, insert a clean knife or wooden skewer into the centre of the cake: it should come out clean.

Allow to cool for 10 minutes outside of the oven. While still warm, brush the top of the cake with whisky. Leave the cake cool completely on a wire cooling rack before wrapping in greaseproof and aluminium foil.

To decorate the cake and board
Unwrap the cake and place it upside down on the smaller cake board. Gently warm the apricot jam and use it to adhere the cake to the board. If there are any gaps between the cake and the board, fill them with small pieces of marzipan. Place the cake and board on a sheet of greaseproof paper. Brush a thin layer of warmed apricot jam over the top and sides of the cake.

On a surface dusted with icing sugar, roll the marzipan out to a thickness of 5mm using spacers. It must be large enough to cover the cake. Using a rolling pin, lift the rolled marzipan and lay it over the cake. Smooth the marzipan over the cake, flattening the top and sides, using your hands. Trim away any excess marzipan using a kitchen knife. Flatten the top and sides of the cake using cake smoothers until even.

Brush some clear alcohol over the marzipan-covered cake to create an adhesive. Roll out the ivory sugar paste and place over the marzipan in the same way. Trim away any excess as before, reserving the trimmings for covering the cake board. Leave to set overnight.

Meanwhile, brush some clear alcohol over the larger cake board. Roll the remaining ivory sugar paste out to a thickness of 3mm and lay over the board. Press down with one of the cake smoothers and trim away any excess leaving a small overlap all around the edges, reserving the trimmings for making the plaque.

Pick up the covered board with one hand and, using your other, push the overlapping sugar

paste down with the smoother until it falls off, creating a clean chamfered edge. Use a kitchen knife with a plain edge to cut off any remaining sugar paste from the sides of the board. Leave to set overnight.

The following day, spread a thin layer of royal icing on the centre of the covered board and place the cake on top. Make sure no icing shows from under the edge. Allow to set for at least 30 minutes.

To decorate the sides of the cake

To recreate the design of the larger cake you need two paper piping bags (see page 184) filled with royal icing at soft-peak consistency (see page 183), one coloured brown and the other coloured ivory. To recreate the design of the smaller cake you need ivory royal icing only.

For the damask design, mix the remaining royal icing with brown soft-peak icing **(1–3)**. For the swag design, mix it with ivory. Hold the stencil tight and flat on the side of the cake **(4)**. If possible, get someone to assist by holding the stencil in place while you spread the icing over the top **(5)**. Once the design is covered **(6)**, carefully remove the stencil **(7)**. Make sure you do not get any icing on the clean sugar paste. Allow to dry. Clean the stencil each time before applying the next pattern onto the cake.

For the brown damask design, outline the details with the ivory soft-peak icing **(8)**. For the ivory swag design, outlines are not required. Once dry, mix the gold lustre with a drop of alcohol and piping gel to create a thick golden paint **(9)**. Use it to paint either the outlines of the damask pattern or the ivory swag detail, using a fine artist's brush **(10)**.

To make the oval plaque

Mix 75g sugar paste with 75g flower paste. If sticky, knead in a small amount of vegetable fat. For the large cake, colour the paste with ivory food colour. For the small cake, colour the paste with brown food colour.

On a surface lightly dusted with icing sugar,

roll the paste out to a thickness of 2mm. Using an oval cutter, cut out an oval and place it on top of a sheet of greaseproof paper. For the larger cake, generously dust the ivory oval plaque with gold lustre. Make sure that the sides are covered as well as the top.

Brush the middle of the cake with a thin layer of clear alcohol. Lay the plaque centred on top.

To make the stag

For the brown stag, mix the remaining flower paste with a small amount of white vegetable fat and brown food colour. For the golden stag, mix the flower paste with ivory food colour. For the brown stag, brush the inside of the stag mould generously with cocoa powder. For the golden stag, brush with gold lustre **(11)**. Make sure all gaps and corners of the mould are covered.

Press the florist's paste inside the mould; use individual pieces for the smaller more delicate areas **(12)**. Rub the back surface of the stag until smooth and to ensure all the pieces of its body are holding together. Trim away any excess paste until the back of the stag is perfectly level **(13–14)**.

To release the stag, bend the mould from the inside out until the stag falls out **(15)**. Allow to dry for a short time. Once the stag feels slightly set, carefully transfer it onto the plaque and stick it down with edible glue.

To pipe a frame around the plaque

Using the piping bag filled with the soft peak icing, pipe a simple C-scroll border around the edge of the plaque. Pipe small teardrops and dots between each scroll to create a pretty design to frame the plaque. To get a feel for the scale and continuity of the piped design, practise the border on a piece of paper first before piping directly onto the cake **(16)**.

If using the ivory icing, paint the border with gold lustre once dry.

Finish the cake with either a satin ribbon or a row of piped dots around the base.

DELICIOUS DRINKS

PINK LEMONADE

OUR PINK LEMONADE IS A FAVOURITE AT THE PARLOUR AND GOES
HAND-IN-HAND WITH A YUMMY CUPCAKE. THE CRANBERRY JUICE PROVIDES THE
PRETTY PINK COLOUR. FOR OTHER VARIATIONS, ADD BLACKCURRANT JUICE
FOR A DEEPER CERISE PINK OR KIWI JUICE FOR A LIGHT GREEN.

Makes approximately 4 glasses

ingredients

100ml freshly squeezed lemon juice
100g caster sugar
500ml water
60ml cranberry or raspberry juice
Ice cubes and lemon slices, to serve

equipment

Juicer or citrus press
Saucepan
Glass jug or teapot
Tall glasses

Place the lemon juice, caster sugar and water in
a saucepan and bring to the boil. Simmer until
the sugar crystals have dissolved, then set aside
to cool.

Once cool, add the cranberry juice.

Serve cold in tall glasses with lots of ice and
slices of fresh lemon.

MINTEANI

A LIGHT AND REFRESHING ICED MINT TEA COCKTAIL
PERFECT FOR A SUMMER PARTY. SERVE IN STYLISH VINTAGE TEACUPS
TO CREATE A SOPHISTICATED YET RELAXED LOOK.

Makes approximately 4 teacups

ingredients

Handful of fresh mint leaves
1 tsp Peggy's Peppermint & Green Tea Leaves
or any other good-quality peppermint tea
150ml water
150ml freshly squeezed lemon juice
150g caster sugar
50ml vodka
A splash of Crème de Menthe
A splash of freshly squeezed lime juice
Ice cubes

equipment

Juicer or citrus press
Saucepan
Glass jug or teapot
(with an infuser, if using loose-leaf tea)
Vintage teacups

Pick the fine leaf tips off the fresh mint twigs and place into iced water to keep them fresh.

Place the remaining mint leaves together with the peppermint tea into a glass jug or teapot.

Bring the water to the boil and pour over the peppermint and green tea leaves. Leave to infuse for 3 minutes. Allow to cool.

Place the lemon juice and caster sugar in a saucepan and bring to the boil. Simmer until the sugar crystals have dissolved, then set aside to cool.

Once the liquids are cool, mix them together and add the vodka, Crème de Menthe and lime juice. Chill.

Serve cold in vintage teacups with ice and the fine leaf tips of fresh mint.

SUMMER BERRY ICE TEA

THIS IS A REFRESHING DRINK, PERFECT FOR A HOT SUMMER'S DAY.

Makes approximately 4 glasses

ingredients

400ml water
4 tsp Peggy's Summer Berry Tea Leaves or any other
good-quality mixed berry tea
Juice of 1 lemon
Juice of 1 orange
50g caster sugar
Ice cubes and fresh mixed summer berries, to serve

equipment

Juicer or citrus press
Glass jug or teapot (with an infuser, if using loose-leaf tea)
Short glasses

Place the summer berry tea leaves into a glass
jug or teapot.

Bring the water to the boil and pour over the
summer berry tea leaves. Leave to infuse for 3–5
minutes. Allow to cool.

Place the lemon, orange juice and caster sugar
in a saucepan and bring to the boil. Simmer until
the sugar crystals have dissolved, then set aside
to cool.

Once the liquids are cool, mix them together.
Chill.

Serve cold in short glasses with ice and a few
fresh summer berries.

HOT WHITE CHOCOLATE WITH VANILLA

A WONDERFUL WINTER WARMER FOR THE SERIOUSLY SWEET-TOOTHED.
SERVE WITH SPICED CHRISTMAS BISCUITS OR JUST ENJOY ON ITS OWN.

Makes approximately 4 glasses

ingredients

150ml whipping cream
300ml milk
Pinch ground nutmeg
Seeds of ½ vanilla pod
150g white chocolate

equipment

Saucepan
Tall glass mugs

Place the cream, milk, nutmeg and vanilla seeds (you can also add the pod but remove it before adding the cream to the chocoate) in a saucepan and bring to a bare simmer.

Place the chocolate in a mixing bowl and pour over the hot cream. Whisk together until the chocolate has melted.

Serve warm in tall glass mugs.

HOME-MADE HOT CHOCOLATE

A CHOCOHOLIC'S DELIGHT! USING REAL CHOCOLATE INSTEAD OF JUST COCOA POWDER MAKES ALL THE DIFFERENCE. THIS IS A SUMPTUOUS RECIPE THAT WILL GIVE YOU AN INSTANT HIT OF HAPPINESS.

Makes approximately 2 mugs or 3–4 teacups

ingredients

125g plain chocolate (minimum 53% cocoa solids),
chopped or in buttons
2 tsp cocoa powder, plus extra
for dusting (optional)
125ml whipping cream
300ml milk
Seeds of ½ vanilla pod

equipment

Saucepan
Teacups
Stencil (optional)

Place the cream, milk and vanilla seeds (you can also add the pod but remove it before adding the cream to the chocolate) in a saucepan and bring to a bare simmer.

Place the chocolate in a mixing bowl and sift in the cocoa powder. Pour over the hot cream. Whisk together until the chocolate has melted.

Return to the saucepan and heat again for a few more minutes while stirring. Do not allow to boil as the chocolate can burn and become bitter. Taste to make sure the cocoa powder has completely dissolved. Pass through a sieve.

Serve warm in teacups.

For a pretty patterned effect, place a small stencil over the rim of the teacup and dust with cocoa powder.

BANANA & PEANUT BUTTER SMOOTHIE

THIS DELICIOUS ENERGISING DRINK IS ENJOYED BY YOUNG AND OLD
AND GREAT FOR USING UP OVER-RIPE BANANAS.
I LOVE DRINKING IT IN THE MORNING AS IT MAKES A QUICK
AND WHOLESOME BREAKFAST.

Makes about 2 glasses

ingredients

2 very ripe bananas
350ml cold milk
1 tbsp smooth peanut butter
1–2 tsp honey (depending on the ripeness of the
bananas)

equipment

Free-standing or hand blender with a jug
Tall glasses
Straws

Place all the ingredients into the jug and blend
until smooth and frothy.

Serve immediately in tall glasses.

MULLED WINE

MULLED WINE IS ONE OF MY FAVOURITE CHRISTMAS TREATS AND REMINDS
ME OF THE WONDERFUL HOURS I HAVE SPENT AT GERMAN CHRISTMAS MARKETS
NEAR MY HOME, STANDING KNEE-DEEP IN SNOW. MULLED WINE, OR GLÜHWEIN AS I CALL IT,
TASTES DELICIOUS WITH TRADITIONAL CHRISTMAS COOKIES SUCH AS MY MULLED
WINE COOKIES (SEE PAGES 52-3) OR GINGERBREAD (SEE PAGES 50–51). FOR A FESTIVE TOUCH,
I SERVE THE MULLED WINE IN UNIQUE VINTAGE TEACUP WINE GLASSES.

Makes about 4 teacups

ingredients

1 orange, plus extra slices for serving
500ml red wine
50ml green ginger wine
100ml water
35g caster sugar
1 tsp cloves, crushed
2 cinnamon sticks, crushed, plus extra
for serving
½ tsp ground nutmeg
1 star anise, crushed, plus extra for serving

equipment

Potato peeler
Saucepan
Fine sieve or muslin
Vintage teacup wine glasses or any other
beautiful heatproof glasses or mugs

Peel the rind from the orange and cut it in half.

Place the orange peel, orange halves and all the other ingredients in a saucepan. Gently warm for about 20 minutes. Do not allow it to boil.

Take the pan off the heat, cover the top with cling film or a lid and leave to infuse for at least 30 minutes.

Once infused, strain through a fine sieve to remove the peel and spices.

Serve warm in vintage teacup wine glasses.

THE ICING
ON THE CAKE

In this chapter I demonstrate the decorating techniques and other finishing touches used to assemble and embellish the cakes and confections throughout this book. It's called The Icing on the Cake because all the techniques and recipes given here will add that touch of finesse to your baking. This chapter is a helpful resource of easy-to-follow tips on making simple sugar blossoms, frosting and icing cakes and cupcakes and making royal icing for piped decorations. As the quantities vary with each recipe, here are some basic ratios and explanations for the most essential ingredients used:

Soft modelling sugar paste On its own sugar paste is too soft for moulding and tears during the process so I mix it with gum tragacanth, which is a tasteless, water-soluble natural gum used as a hardening or thickening agent. The ratio is roughly 1 tsp gum tragacanth to 300g sugar paste, depending on the required stiffness. It does tend to make the sugar paste a little dry, so add a dab of white vegetable fat to make the paste smooth and pliable again. Once mixed, the sugar paste needs to rest for about 30 minutes to firm up. As the paste dries out quickly when exposed to air it should be covered with cling film or placed in a plastic bag.

Edible glue You can by ready-made edible glue, but I tend to make mine by mixing 1 tsp gum tragacanth with 150ml water. You can also use CMC instead of gum tragacanth. At first the mixture will be lumpy but, when stirred occasionally, the powder will slowly swell and combine with the water to make a smooth and thick gel. If it stiffens too much, just add a little more water. The consistency should be a bit softer than hair gel. I use edible glue to stick together sugar paste or flower paste.

Royal icing You can buy ready-made royal icing sugar, which is icing sugar pre-mixed with powdered egg white, and all you have to do is add water. These mixes work very well but can be a little costly. I make my royal icing from sifted cane icing sugar as it is finer than beet icing sugar. The ratio of icing sugar to liquid egg white (be it fresh, pasteurised or powdered mixed with water) is 6:1. So for 3kg icing sugar you need 500ml liquid. This is a good guide for a general recipe that you can scale up or down as required. When making royal icing, it is crucial that all your equipment is grease-free as otherwise the icing will not propertly stiffen. Likewise take great care not to get any yolk in with your white when separating your eggs.

basic baking kit

Free-standing electric mixer with whisk
and paddle attachment, for example
from Kitchen Aid or Kenwood
Food processor or hand blender
A set of different sized mixing bowls
Measuring jug
Rubber spatula
Pastry brush with natural or synthetic bristles
(silicon brushes do not pick up enough liquid)
Selection of baking trays
Large non-stick rolling pin
Pair of marzipan spacers
Fine sieve for dusting and sifting flour and
icing sugar
Small and large palette knife
Sharp pair of scissors
Cake leveller or long serrated kitchen knife
Small plain edged kitchen knife
Wire cooling rack
Deep saucepan
Metal disc or other flat disc
(such as the loose base of a springform cake tin)
Non-slip tilting turntable
Plastic piping bags
Cling film
Silicon or greaseproof paper

SIMPLE DAISIES & LEAVES

you will need

White sugar paste
White vegetable fat
Yellow and green paste food colour
Petal dust (optional)
Small amount of royal icing mixed to soft-peak consistency and coloured to a pale yellow shade (see page 183)

equipment

Small non-stick plastic board with non-slip mat
Small non-stick plastic rolling pin
Daisy plunge cutter, or similar
Small leaf cutter
Dresden or veining tool
Perforated foam pad
Plastic artist's palette with 10 wells, or use perforated foam pad
Fine artist's brush (optional)
Paper piping bag (see page 184)

To make a daisy Knead the sugar paste with a small amount of white vegetable fat until smooth and pliable. Roll out the paste to a thickness of approximately 2mm.

Place the daisy cutter on the paste and press firmly. Lift off the cutter and, using your fingers, clean up the petal edges. Release the daisy from the cutter on to the foam pad. Using the veining tool, score down the centre of each petal. Place the daisy in a well of the palette or on the foam pad and leave to set.

To add a yellow centre to the daisy, use a paper piping bag filled with pale yellow royal icing in a soft-peak consistency. Pipe a small dot in the centre of the flower. Leave to dry.

To make a leaf Knead the sugar paste with a small amount of green paste food colour and then white vegetable fat until smooth and pliable. Roll out the green paste to a thickness of approximately 2mm.

Place the small leaf cutter firmly on the green paste and press. Lift off the cutter and release the leaf from the cutter on to the foam pad. Using the veining tool, score down the centre of the leaf to create a curved shape. Leave on the foam pad to set.

QUICK & EASY BLOSSOMS

you will need

White sugar paste coloured with paste food colour, as required
White vegetable fat
Petal dust (optional)
Small amount of royal icing mixed to a soft-peak consistency (see page 183)

equipment

Small non-stick plastic board with non-slip mat
Small non-stick plastic rolling pin
Blossom cutter
Blossom veiner
Plastic artist's palette with 10 wells, or use perforated foam pad
Fine artist's brush (optional)
Paper piping bag (optional)

Knead the sugar paste with a small amount of paste food colour, if using, and then white vegetable fat until smooth and pliable. Roll out the paste to a thickness of approximately 2mm.

Place the blossom cutter on the paste and press firmly. Lift off the cutter and release the blossom. Cut a few at a time. Lightly grease the blossom veiner with white vegetable fat. One by one, place each blossom shape in the veiner and press. Carefully bend the veiner outwards to release the shaped blossom and place in a well of a palette or on a foam pad. Leave to set for at least a few hours or preferably overnight.

Once dry, you can add shades of colour to your blossoms by brushing with a tiny amount of petal dust using a fine artist's brush. If required, pipe a small dot of icing in the centre of the blossom and leave to dry.

CHRYSANTHEMUMS

you will need

White sugar paste coloured with paste food colour, as required
Gum tragacanth
White vegetable fat
Chrysanthemum silicon mould (I use one from First Impressions)

Knead the sugar paste with small amounts of gum tragacanth until firm and pliable. Add the food colour to achieve the required shade. If the paste feels sticky, add a small amount of white vegetable fat. Wrap the paste in cling film and leave for 15–30 minutes to firm up.

Rub a thin layer of white vegetable fat over the mould. Press a walnut-sized piece of paste firmly into the mould. Smooth the surface with a palette knife and clean up the edges with your fingers. Carefully bend the mould outwards to release the flower.

RICE-PAPER BLOSSOMS

you will need

Sheets of edible rice paper
Edible pearl lustre spray in pink, blue and green
Flower paper punch

Spray the rice paper with the edible pearl lustre and leave to dry for a few minutes. Keep the rice paper as flat as possible as the spray will make it curl slightly.

Using the paper punch, cut out the flower shapes.

APPLIQUÉ BLOSSOMS

you will need

White sugar paste coloured with paste food colour, a required
Gum tragacanth
White vegetable fat
A small amount of clear alcohol, such as vodka, or edible glue (see page 172)

equipment

Small non-stick plastic board with non-slip mat
Small non-stick plastic rolling pin
Selection of blossom cutters in different shapes and sizes
Fine artist's brush

Knead the sugar paste with small amounts of gum tragacanth until firm and pliable. Add the food colour to achieve the required shade then knead in a small amount of vegetable fat until smooth and pliable. Roll out the paste to a thickness of approximately 2mm. When not in use, wrap the paste in cling film to prevent it drying out. Place a blossom cutter on the paste and press firmly. Lift off the cutter and release the blossom. Cut as many different shapes, sizes and colours as required. Brush a small amount of clear alcohol or edible glue on to a large blossom and place a medium-sized blossom on top. Layer as many different sizes and colours together as required. Leave to slightly set before applying to the cake.

tip

The appliqué blossoms should be set enough that they hold their shape, but pliable enough that you can place them on curved surfaces without the paste cracking.

AUTUMN LEAVES

you will need

Marzipan
White vegetable fat
Edible copper and gold lustre powder

equipment

Autumn leaf silicon mould
(I use one from First Impressions)
Small non-stick plastic rolling pin
Large soft powder brush
Perforated foam pad to dry leaves

Make the leaves at least one day ahead of use to allow them enough time to set. Knead the marzipan until smooth and pliable. Rub a thin layer of white vegetable fat over the mould. Place a walnut-sized piece of marzipan into the mould and, using a rolling pin, press down until the marzipan covers the leaf design. Flatten and smooth the surface with your fingers until it is an even thickness, then trim away any excess marzipan with a kitchen knife. Carefully bend the mould outwards to release the leaf. Place the leaf on a small piece of greaseproof paper. For an autumnal effect, brush the leaf with a mixture of edible copper and gold lustre powder. Transfer the leaf to a foam flower pad and leave to set.

tip

I use marzipan rather than sugar paste for these leaves as its natural oil enhances the metallic lustre. If too soft, knead in a little icing sugar or gum tragacanth into the marzipan until firm.

FROSTING CUPCAKES
USING A PIPING BAG AND ROUND NOZZLE

Whether you are using a plain round nozzle or a star nozzle, the technique for piping frosting on to cupcakes is the same.

To prepare the plastic piping bag, snip the tip to make an opening large enough for the nozzle. Fit the nozzle then fill the piping bag with frosting that is soft but still cool enough to hold its shape when piped. Twist the open end of the bag closed and hold it in a fist to prevent the frosting from oozing out the top.

Hold the piping bag vertically with the nozzle close to the centre of the cupcake. Squeeze the bag until the frosting comes out: the pressure should be coming from your fist. Hold the tip of the piping bag steady with your free hand. As the frosting spreads, move the nozzle from the centre of the cupcake to around the outside while squeezing at a steady pressure.

When you have gone once around the outside of the cupcake, slowly come back to the centre. Pipe another layer over the first one.

Once you reach the centre of the cupcake, stop squeezing, then lightly push the nozzle down into the frosting just a few millimetres and lift the nozzle off. This motion creates a perfect peak to the frosting.

Once the frosting has been piped on top, chill the cupcakes for 15–30 minutes to set before adding your chosen decoration.

using a piping bag and star nozzle

FROSTING CUPCAKES
USING A SMALL PALETTE KNIFE

Make sure the frosting is soft and spreadable.

Pile the equivalent of two palette-knives worth of frosting onto the top of the cupcake. Using a palette knife, spread the frosting over the top of the cupcake, scraping the palette knife straight down the edge of the paper cake case.

Using the palette knife, spread the frosting sideways around the top of the cupcake, slightly flattening the top but retaining the dome shape.

To finish, sweep the palette knife once around the sides of the cupcake along the ege of the paper cake case and then lift off.

Once the frosting has been spread on top, chill the cupcakes for 15–30 minutes to set before adding your chosen decoration.

1 **2** **3** **4** **5** **6** **7** **8** **9** **10** **11** **12** **13** **14** **15** **16**

ASSEMBLING LAYER CAKES

you will need

Cake leveller or large serrated knife
Non-slip turntable
Flat metal disc that is larger than the turntable
(I use the loose base of a springform cake tin)
Cake card the same size and shape as the cake
Pastry brush and jug (if the recipe requires sugar syrup)
Large flat palette knife
Metal side scraper

1 Evenly trim the tops of all the cake layers using either a cake leveller or large serrated knife.

2 Discard the trimmings. For light sponges, also trim the bottom off the middle layer to remove any dark crumb: this is not required for a dark chocolate cake. If any dark crumb is left on top of the cake after trimming, rub the surface in a circular motion using your hand held flat until the majority of the darker crumbs have come off.

3 Centre a flat metal disc on top of a non-slip turntable, then place the cake card in the middle, securing it to the disc with a dab of buttercream or ganache. Spread a thin layer of buttercream or ganache over the cake card.

4 Lay the bottom cake layer on the cake card with the crumb side facing downwards. If required by the recipe, brush the cake layer with sugar syrup.

5 Spoon the filling onto the middle of the cake layer. Using a large flat palette knife, spread the filling evenly outwards from the middle by turning the turntable against the direction of the palette knife. Hold the palette knife edge parallel with the cake, but with the blade tilting upwards slightly. Spread the filling evenly to a thickness of approximately 3–5mm.

6 Lay the middle cake layer on top of the bottom layer; for a light sponge, this is the layer that has been trimmed on both top and bottom. If required by the recipe, brush the cake layer with sugar syrup.

7 Spread the filling over this middle cake layer, as in step 5, then lay the top cake layer on top of the middle layer with the crumb side facing upwards. Press down gently with your hand held flat to remove any air pockets between the layers.

8 Spoon a generous amount of buttercream, frosting or ganache on top of the cake.

9 Using a large flat palette knife, spread the buttercream, frosting or ganache over the surface of the cake as in step 5. Apply enough pressure to spread the coating thinly until the dark crumb shows through and the excess coating overlaps the edges.

10 Holding the palette knife vertically, push the overlapping coating down the sides of the cake. Spread the coating sideways using a back-and-forth paddling motion while turning the turntable against the direction of the palette knife.

11 Once the cake is covered, take a metal side scraper all round the sides in a single swoop to get them as straight as possible. Again, this should be a very thin layer that allows the dark crumb to show through.

12 Clean the top surface of the cake by scraping any excess coating from the edges towards the middle using the palette knife in a 'flicking' motion. This first coat is called the crumb coat; its purpose is to hold any crumbs together and create a basic shape for the cake. The better the crumb coat, the better the final result. Chill the cake until the crumb coat has set, this may between 30 minutes and 1 hour.

13–14 For the final masking coat, cover the cake top and sides with clean, crumb-free buttercream, frosting or ganache as in steps 9 and 10. Use enough coating so that no crumbs show through. You will need to work fast at this stage as the chilled crumb coat underneath will quickly set the fresh masking coat.

15 Once the top and sides of the cake are masked, run a metal side scraper all round the sides in a single swoop as in step 11, holding the bottom edge of the side scraper against the cake card. If the results are not perfect the first time, repeat this step as it requires a little practise.

16 Clean the top surface of the cake as in step 12. Chill the cake in the fridge for at least 1 hour or until set.

ROYAL ICING

ingredients

Icing sugar, sifted (see page 172)
Squeeze of lemon juice
Egg white or Meri-White powdered egg white (mixed with water as per the
instructions on the packet)

equipment

Electric mixer with paddle attachment
Rubber spatula
Medium-sized bowl or plastic food storage container with lid
Clean damp cloth
Cling film (optional)

Place the icing sugar in the clean and grease-free bowl of an electric mixer together with the lemon juice and three-quarters of the egg white or Meri-White.

Mix on the lowest speed until combined. You may want to cover the mixing bowl with a cloth to prevent icing sugar dust from going everywhere. If the mixture looks too dry, add a little more liquid until the icing looks smooth but not wet. After approximately 2 minutes, scrape the sides of the bowl to make sure the icing is well combined. Should the mixture still look too dry and grainy along the edges, add a little more liquid. Should the icing look slightly runny and glossy, adjust the consistency by adding a little bit more sifted icing sugar.

Continue mixing at the lowest speed for 4–5 minutes. Keep an eye on the consistency as royal icing can easily become overworked and overly aerated if mixed too long.

The royal icing is ready when stiff peaks appear around the sides of the bowl and you can hear a sloshing sound as the paddle moves the icing around. The icing should be smooth and satin-like in texture.

Transfer into a clean bowl or plastic food storage container and cover with a clean damp cloth. The icing can be stored for up to 1 week at room temperature if covered with a lid or cling film.

FILLING A PIPING BAG WITH ROYAL ICING

When filling a paper piping bag with royal icing, use approximately 1 tablespoon at a time. The cleanest way to fill a bag is use a palette knife, scraping the icing down the folded edge of the piping bag and letting it drop inside. With a clean palette knife, carefully push the icing down the bag as far as possible.

Once filled, flatten the open end of the piping bag with the seam centred on one side.

Fold the top of the piping bag over, away from the seam, and keep folding until you cannot fold any further to create tension on the bag; this tension will make it easier to pipe.

Store the filled piping bag in a re-sealable plastic bag until ready to use. Once ready to pipe, snip a small section straight across the tip of the bag using a pair of sharp scissors.

tip

After being stored for a few days, the liquid and icing may separate. If this occurs, place the icing in the bowl of an electric mixer and mix on the lowest speed to bring it back together.

COLOUR & CONSISTENCY

you will need

Royal icing
Small palette knife
Jug filled with water
Clean smooth worksurface or flat disc for mixing, or use a small bowl
Paste or liquid food colour
Cling film or re-sealable plastic bag (optional)

COLOURING ROYAL ICING

1 Place the royal icing onto a clean surface or flat disc next to a small amount of food colour. Using a palette knife, pick up small amount of royal icing and mix it with the food colour.

2 Work the food colour through the icing, breaking down any tiny colour specs as, if not mixed properly, these can burst and bleed as the icing dries.

3 Once mixed, add the coloured icing a little at a time to the white icing and blend until you have achieved the required shade.

CONSISTENCY OF ROYAL ICING

4 To make soft-peak royal icing, dip the palette knife into water and mix it through until the icing looks a little glossy and forms peaks that fall over, yet still hold their shape. This consistency is for piping outlines, borders and dots as well as for stencilling work.

5 To make runny royal icing, keep adding water until the icing looks shiny, flows together and flattens within 4–6 seconds. This consistency is perfect for flooding cookies.

MAKING A PAPER PIPING BAG

Take a rectangular piece of silicon or waxed greaseproof paper – approximately 30cm x 45cm (12in x 18in) – and cut it in half diagonally from one corner to the opposite corner. Rather than making a series of snips, slide the blades of the scissors through the paper to make a cleaner cut.

Hold one of the resulting paper triangles with your hand at the middle of the longest side and with your hand on the point on the opposite side. The longer side of the triangle should be on your left.

1 Curl the shorter corner on your right over to the corner that is pointing towards you, so that it forms a cone.

2 With your left hand, wrap the longer corner on the left around the tip of the cone twice.

3 Join the corner together with the other two corners at the back of the cone.

4 If the bag has an open tip at the point of the cone, close it by adjusting and tightening the inner and outer layers. Wiggle the layers back and forth until the cone forms a sharp point.

5 Fold the corners at the open end into the inside of the bag twice to prevent it unravelling.

tip

When filling, only ever half-fill the piping bag otherwise the contents will ooze out when you squeeze. Once half-full, close the bag by folding the side with the seam over to the plain side twice.

PIPING TECHNIQUES

The piping techniques demonstrated above are very useful to practise your general piping skills. Instead of piping directly onto a cookie or cake, simply take a piece of greaseproof paper and pipe on to that instead. You can also place templates underneath it and trace them through the paper with your piping bag. If you have never piped with royal icing before, this task is a great way to train your skills, after all practice makes perfect.

First snip a small tip off your piping bag already filled with icing. Hold the bag between the thumb and the fingers of your preferred hand; place your thumb over the folded end of the bag so that the bag stays firmly closed and place your index finger along the seam at the back of the bag. Use the index finger of your other hand to guide the nozzle.

PIPING LINES

Holding your bag at a 45°angle to the surface, touch the starting point with the tip of the bag and slowly squeeze out the icing. As you are squeezing, lift the bag up about 2.5cm (1in) and guide the line straight towards you or, for example, along the sides of a cookie. Once you are approaching the finishing point, gradually bring the bag down, stop squeezing and lay the line by touching the finishing point with the tip of the bag. This is called the lifting method.

PIPING DOTS

Hold the tip of your piping bag 1mm above the surface and squeeze out the icing to produce a dot on the surface. Keep the tip low inside the dot and allow the dot to spread to the required size. Once the dot has reached the required size, stop squeezing and lift off the tip while flicking it in a circular motion. Should the dot form a little peak at the top, flatten it carefully with a damp artist's brush.

PIPING LOOPS AND SWAGS

Start as you would for piping lines. Holding your bag almost vertically to the surface, touch the starting point with the tip and slowly squeeze out the icing. As you squeeze, lift the bag up by about 2.5cm (1in) and move it from one side to the other in circular movements, overlapping the lines in even intervals to create evenly spaced loops and swags.

tip

If you find it difficult to space the loops and swags out evenly, mark the points where the loops will meet and use them as guides.

THANK YOU

I have taken so much pride in writing this book, from the initial concept to creating the recipes and photographing at the Peggy Porschen Parlour, that I have cherished every single minute.

From the bottom of my heart, I would like to thank everyone who has helped to make **Boutique Baking** possible. As always, it has been a great team effort and I could not have done it without the help of some very special people.

I would like to thank my publisher and the team at Quadrille Publishing, Alison Cathie, Jane O'Shea, Helen Lewis and Lisa Pendreigh for their shared enthusiasm and support in creating this book. As always, it's been wonderful working with you.

A big thank you to my favourite photographer, Georgia Glynn Smith, who has once again created magical pictures. To the very talented stylist Vicky Sullivan, for setting the perfect scene for my cakes. And to Helen Bratby for designing this beautiful book. I'm so glad you all have been part of the team as I could not have done it without you.

I also would like to thank the wonderful artist Carol Gillott for coming on board and providing such a beautiful illustration for the front cover. I have been a fan of her work for such a long time and I am thrilled to be working with her.

I would like to thank Mark Shipley for his invaluable guidance and business expertise. My colleague Stephanie Balls for assisting me with the initial concept for **Boutique Baking** and for always being at hand when I'm lost for words. A massive thank you goes to my talented baker Marianne Stewart, who has played a key role in developing some of the most delicious recipes in this book. And to my talented team of cake decorators, Cinthia Panariello, Franziska Thomczik, Maxie Giertz, Naomi Lee, and Nicola Fürle, who have all been invaluable throughout the entire production.

Thanks to my lovely retail angels, Zane Sniedze, Laura McGowan, Patience Harding, Reena Mathen and Theresa Thomczik who all brightened up the pages with their beautiful smiles.

A big thank you goes to our model, the lovely Eleanor Jones for eating more Ice Cream Cake Pops than any child at this age should and to Javier and Toni of By Appointment Only Design for contributing the most beautiful flower arrangements.

I would also like to take this as a special opportunity to thank the entire team at Peggy Porschen Cakes, it's been a fantastic first year and you have all helped in making the Parlour the best place to eat cake in London. Well that's what I think anyway. I feel blessed to have such a talented and enthusiastic team and I truly cherish working with all of you.

A very special thank you goes to my lovely great aunt Anita Leibel and her grandson Fabian, both have been tirelessly collecting the most beautiful vintage china pieces, many of which I have used as props in this book. Since, I have become so hooked on the whole vintage china thing and my collection is ever-growing.

I would like to thank my dad, Lee Pollock, Toni Franken, Brian Ma Siy and Chalkley Calderwood for helping to turn my creative vision for the Parlour into reality and all of our suppliers who have supported us right from the start.

A heartfelt thank you to all of our customers, past and present, for your support and trust which has helped grow Peggy Porschen Cakes from a small business to the brand it is today.

Last but certainly not least, an overwhelming amount of gratitude goes to my family, for giving me all the strength and support I could ever wish for and more.

SUPPLIERS

Most of the equipment and ingredients used to create the cakes and confections in this book are available from specialist cake decorating suppliers and, increasingly, the more everyday items can be found in supermarkets and general cookware shops.

My own website – **www.peggyporschen.com** – includes an online shop where you can purchase specialist cake decorating tools and ingredients, as well as an assortment of cookie cutters and other bakeware products. In addition, there is a small selection of handmade jams and exclusive loose-leaf tea blends available from Peggy's Pantry.

Throughout each year, I run a series of classes at the Peggy Porschen Academy. So whether you want to perfect your piping techniques to create irresistible cookies or brush up your baking skills to make heavenly cupcakes decorated with posies of spring flowers, there is a suitable course.

Each morning my team of specialist bakers freshly bake a range of layer cakes, cupcakes, cookies and other yummy delights for visitors to the Peggy Porschen Parlour to either enjoy there and then with an artisan tea blend or coffee or to take away for a teatime treat. If you have enjoyed the recipes in this book, I hope you will pay us a visit.

Peggy Porschen Academy
30 Elizabeth Street
Belgravia
London SW1W 9RB
www.peggyporschen.com

Peggy Porschen Parlour
116 Ebury Street
Belgravia
London SW1W 9QQ
www.peggyporschen.com

INDEX